THIS TIME AROUND

PASSAGES

John T. Eber Sr.

MANAGING EDITOR

A publication of

Eber & Wein Publishing

Pennsylvania

This Time Around: Passages
Copyright © 2013 by Eber & Wein Publishing as a compilation.

Library of Congress
Cataloging in Publication Data

ISBN 978-1-60880-277-7

Proudly manufactured in the United States of America by

Eber & Wein Publishing
Pennsylvania

TO MY DEAR FRIEND IRENE
NOVEMBER 28, 2013
Don

A Note from the Editor . . .

"In books I have traveled, not only to other worlds, but into my own."
    –Anna Quindlen, *How Reading Changed My Life*

Everyone who has ever had the privilege to possess a book has held a passport in his or her own hands, and everyone who has ever had the pleasure of reading has traveled more places than he or she could ever reach on foot as a consequence of deep meditation. Readers young and old rarely know exactly where a book will take them before cracking its spine, but they are usually confident embarking on a journey beginning in bound form will be significantly more affordable, convenient, relaxing and rewarding than many physical ventures. Voyages through verse in anthologies such as *This Time Around* are guaranteed to be substantially more varied than typical travel; and they are just as, if no more so, unearthing as many places our own two feet can take us. If a book is a passport, its content seemingly provides the evidential stamp of the reader's adventure. Be prepared: this collection of exquisite and extensive literary talent will take you to places you have never imagined, beyond the barriers of your personal experience and worldview to eclectic settings and situations you potentially have yet to even envisage. Deservingly, reading this array of dynamic poetics will also lead you deep into your own existence—allowing you to relate to other poets through the representations of human experience they have so carefully crafted, and causing you to reassess your own intuition, understanding and judgment of particular phenomenon of life through a newly heightened awareness of humanity.

As Anna Quindlen, American author, journalist, and Pulitzer Prize-winning opinion columnist for the *New York Times* notes, books take us "not only to other worlds, but also into [our] own" in ways only aesthetic experience affords. Because reading causes us to examine ourselves—our pasts, presents and futures, our loves, losses and limitations and our overall human condition—collections of poetry prove invaluable. Sadly, our busy lives often prevent us from seriously considering *ourselves*: our personal histories and how our living biographies are continually shaped by whatever we have done or whatever has been done unto us, whatever we are currently in the act of doing and whatever we hope or fear to engender in days to come. Furthermore, a disappointing handful of people are mindful enough of how social consciousness necessarily cultivates knowledge of self. Admirably and gratefully, poets are some of the chosen few who essentially realize this; even more impressively, poets propagate greater appreciation of this awareness through the dissemination of their individual accounts in poetry.

Thankfully, one of literature's innate advantages is found on each page of every book, in the way each page commands a reader to pause and perceive what he or she has just read. The kind of self-reflection fostered by literature is priceless, because it takes us to a place of understanding and—willingly, eventually— peace. Hopefully, this compilation will excite your own reflections. While thoughtfully consuming all the provoking poetic narratives collected within these pages, make sure to ask yourself: Where will your reading take you *this time around?*

Rachel Rogers
Editor

Taking a Walk

I take a walk every day,
Try to keep in shape that way.
I walk along a road named Walker,
Maybe stop to visit with a neighbor talker.
I love to watch the wild flowers as they grow
Along the sides of the road, you know.
It's very interesting to see what's new,
In the neighbor's yard, what flowers grew,
Especially in the spring when birds appear,
And to feel the sun's warmth all year.
The distance I walk is a mile and a half.
Sometimes the cow down the road has a calf.
Summer walking is the time to wear a hat.
Watching me is my neighbor's cat.
When fall comes and the leaves change,
Their colors have a very wide range.
So what could I do but gather a few,
They're so beautiful in their colorful hue.
Pretty soon I have to wear a jacket,
Wear a toque and zip up the placket.
The holidays come along with the snow,
Have to stay home sometimes, you know.
Sometimes the weather is zero degrees.
To stay in I surely agree.
But pretty soon along comes spring—
I can walk again and my feet take wing.

Barbara King
Clarksburg, MA

My Grandparents

My grandparents spoil me a lot,
So much they could fill up a whole parking lot!
They would do anything, even fly to the moon.
I'm gonna see them pretty soon.

She takes me to the park,
Even with my dad Mark.
She sends me a lot of packages,
Inside there was a book with a secret passage.

She takes me to visit everyone at my old school,
Then we would go to the pool..
She makes the best food,
It's so delicious and good.

I'm going to her house,
She told me to help her catch a mouse.
But she got mad at me because I didn't catch it at all,
So, Tony hit me with a ball!

Joey Shears
Youngstown, OH

My name is Joeseph Isaac Shears. I was born on August 11, 2002 in Westerville, Ohio. I have three siblings, and two step siblings: Kaitlynn (stepsister), Zach (stepbrother), Halia (sister), and Tony (brother). We argue here and there but we get along pretty well. I have the best family in the world. My dad, Mark, was married twice and my stepmom, Timeka, was married twice, so we're The Brady Bunch. We also have two ferrets, Scooter and Casey. I was on my way to my grandparents' house, which inspired me to write the poem.

A Survivor's Journey

The doctor tells you,
"You have cancer"
Shock and fear take hold
So much left unsaid and undone
Sinking into the darkness of the "unknown"
The surgeries
The treatments
The nausea
The pain
The feeling of meeting your maker
Will I ever rise above?
A feeling of helplessness
But you continue to make your way
In hoping the next day is a better day
And when you have a better day,
You begin to see it can be possible
And heaven's door
Seems to become further away
So you start to believe
I will beat this "monster"
And a new perspective on life develops ...
The unknown becomes clearer
Hopelessness begins to subside
And a feeling of survival begins to emerge

Candace L. Fresch
Denver, CO

Peace

Oh, sweet time when there was a brook and I could float my sticks
And breathe the air in the lazy sun of never-ending days; when
Dreams were dreams, and the grass was my bed and the sculptured
Clouds were set in the faintest of blue; and the essence of wild
Things perfumed the air. Days of silence: where uninterrupted
Bliss soaked my skin, where darkness dared not intervene, where
Excitement riddled my every quake, fulfilling all the needs of
Time, when the mind knew no sorrow and the horizon was belief.
Oh, these days I pray will come again when I was very young.

William L. Conley
Madison, CT

I started writing poetry this year. I have completed two hundred and seventy-five poems in nine months. I entered this contest because the people who have read my poems advised me to do so. They stated the poems moved them like the great poets of the past, they were extremely profound. I have composed poems for this day and age that are not included here. I am a foster child, went to school until the third grade. My poems are profound and religious in nature. You have to read them two or three times to get the true meaning

A Moment in Time

It's in that unexpected moment when it strikes.
That flashing instant encompassing
Perplexity,
Relief,
Sheer enchantment.

At first you panic
Because you never once fathomed
How rapidly time could alter
Everything you grew accustomed to,
Without you even being aware of the transition.

Then, you feel at ease
Because you suddenly realize
How truly far you have embarked along
In this unfamiliar journey.

Yet somehow, in the midst of all the disarray,
You're caught up in this powerful sense of bewilderment
For the endless possibilities that your future
Eagerly holds.

So before it is too late,
Remember to never be fearful
Of the uncharted territory that awaits.
Terrifying at first—like all new encounters,
The courage you unknowingly possess
Will find a way to make the uncertainties of this life worth it.

Caroline Laganas
Colorado Springs, CO

Bundy on Exit

The rain performs a concert as
They come I believed until this
Moment it was just a trap of time
As instant as coffee drunk questions
Revolve frantically around and the
Sense it conveys is as honest as the
Lie of today so shudder as the legs
And head are shaved and dress me in my
Sunday best for this final complicated
Game of whatever you desire and in this
Ending moment will I see my naked reflection
Or will I slobber and scream as the blue
Puppeteer descends to make me dance for
His delight releasing all my bodily fluids?

Susan Romano
Irvine, CA

If Only

If only time would tell what the future beholds.
If only I wouldn't be standing out there in the cold.
If only love would come right through.
If only that one standing there would be you.
If only love would pour my feelings out.
If only someone would show me what love was all about.
If only life would be what I thought.
If only true happiness wouldn't have to be something bought.
If only I could look up at the stars and fly.
If only life would never be a lie.
If only true dreams would give a glimpse of what your destiny would be.
If only they would help you to go out there and be free.
If only my direction in life was placed in my hand.
If only this was something I 'd understand.
If only the world would go back and see
that the years before now were the best they would ever be.
If only love would have the sincerity and passion as it once did.
If only those feelings were out there and not hid.
Now, if only I would see what I will achieve,
then and only then will I believe.

Alesha Brooke Norman
Valdese, NC

My name is Alesha Brooke Norman, and I am twenty-three years old. My whole life has been based upon "what if" or "if only" perspectives. I always wanted to do things but never had the courage to stand out there and achieve them. I guess I wanted someone to point me in the right direction so I'd see the true light. But realizing that I had to make the decisions on my own scared me and made me wonder if it'd all become something real. The world had changed so much from when I was a little girl and I guess I wanted to tell myself "if only" it was this way again. But now I see that we have to make the choice and not say "if only." We have to believe in ourselves and have faith that we will make the right decisions. I use that now and I'll hold onto it as I walk down this path in life.

Levi

I see the wonder in his eyes and begin to dream of him in color
What great things of him will arise?
He is but yet still a mere butterfly's flutter

Many faces surface at times when he smiles and I see her and them
Then I see my God's eyes and know this is how it was always meant
I fear though of my actions that I know he will soon understand
I pray to walk correctly while we both walk hand in hand

I want him to know me like the fish swim the sea
like the birds' wings recognize the air
like each heart knows each beat

I want to tell him about love when he first sees it in her eyes
I want to show him how to stand his ground the moment he'll have to
    fight
I want to hold him close when the pain becomes too much inside
I want to tell him that it's okay, that there is no shame to cry

I want to be the man I know I was always meant to be
I want him to love me and see me proudly as a son should always see
His father tall and grand and loving always unconditionally
I'll always be there for him like sweet honey to a bee

Christopher E. Chacon
Federal Way, WA

Old Glory

At sunup a flag is raised
To the top of a pole so high
To wave in the breeze that comes
As Old Glory looks to the sky—

With colors oh so bright,
The red, the white and the blue,
A banner for all to honor—
And our feelings for it should be true.

It's been with our troops in battle,
And at home it always remains
A symbol for all Americans.
Old Glory is its name.

Stripes represent the first thirteen states
With the color of red and white hue,
And each of the fifty states
Has a star in the field of blue.

The stars and stripes are in a parade
As the units go marching by.
Respect it for what it means.
May Old Glory always fly on high.

Mildred O. Oles
Girard, KS

I am a single, retired school board clerk, and, at one time before unification, served as clerk for two boards working for forty-seven years. I had never written a poem until, in middle school, the teacher gave an assignment to write a poem. Surprisingly, I came up with one. After becoming a board clerk, I also served a few years as a sponsor for the high school annual. Two years I wrote poetry to introduce the theme. After moving to a retirement complex, words started rolling out. Eber & Wein has published one of my poems in each of four poetry anthology books.

Wave Our Flag with Pride

We can be proud we are Americans
Because of Veterans like my Dad.
They fought for love of country;
For that we can be glad.
How many lost their lives
And never got to see?
Because they fought for glory,
The rest of us are free.
Peace is born from men like Dad
Who put their lives aside
So we can live each day
And wave our flag with pride.

Marcia Keck Cline
Defiance, OH

Marcia J. (Keck) Cline resides in Defiance, OH, with her husband Dennis and their four Yorkshire Terriers. She is a registered nurse in ICU at Promedica Defiance Regional Hospital in Defiance. She has dedicated her career to helping others and writes poetry to soothe the soul. "Wave Our Flag with Pride" was written in honor of her father, Keith C. Keck, a US Navy World War II veteran, and to all veterans alive and dead.

Moonlight Walk

The moon shown in my window as I lay awake in my bed.
The thoughts of the day fill my weary head.

I wonder what tomorrow will bring and will I be okay?
Can I make it through alone? Will I find my way?

A whisper came on the breeze and found me in my bed.
He said, "Child, I will light your path and you are not alone.
I've come to walk with you tonight to show you your way home."

He called me from my bed and stood me to my feet.
He said, "I've heard your nightly cry; it's time that we should meet."

He showed me how He had been with me to guide me through my
day.
Even in my darkest hour His light did shine my way.

We walked on the moonlit path that led around my home.
He said, "If you invite Me in your house, you will never be alone."

He said, "Rest your faith on Me; I was made to last.
I will be here for your children; I've been here in the past.

So, if you ever feel alone and your world is filled with gloom,
just go to the window and look at the night sky and remember our walk
with the moon."

Daniel J. Miller
Polk, PA

Never Thought I'd See the Day

Never thought I'd see the day, when, in school
you couldn't pray, or mention God in any way.
Never thought I'd see the day, when the ten
commandments were taken down, from public
places across our town.
Never thought I'd see the day, when students
were shot down in the school, and violence
and bullying became more prevalent as a rule.
Signs painted on buildings that say, "There is
no God," along the public streets, we trod.
They are taking "God" away and out of our
lives everyday. Never thought I'd see the day.
The world can't see the disadvantages of
taking "God" out of life everyday, will
only cause wrack and ruin, and, our life will
be in moral decay.
Never thought I'd see the day, God bless
America, of the USA
We all need to pray!

Margaret Ruby
Ottumwa, IA

In Praise of Marias

Some came from Saltillo,
Durango and SanLuis Potosi.
Others from places farther away.

They did not cross oceans
Like nannies abroad.
They forded a river and
Came to our door.

"*Como te llamas?*" My father would ask.
"Just call me Maria," she answered
And we would leave it at that.

They washed, they ironed, swept every room.
They cooked three meals a day
Every morning they braided my sister's hair.
We plotted, we schemed
And there was Maria, hot at our heels.

We took them to movies
We took them to church.
Together we wept at my mother's wake.

"What can they teach your children?"
My uncle would ask.
"The learning, *hermano*," my father answered,
"Will not come from books."

Did I ever tell you, Maria
You live in my heart.
We thank God for Marias
My sister and I.

Angeles Gaona Garza
Brownsville, TX

I Am Woman

I am woman, let me roar when it is my time to roar
Sometimes I need to say exactly what I think
or feel sometimes, sometimes not.

I am woman, let me be silent to meditate
to deliberate on what I must be doing.
Silence can be a golden space for me.

I am woman, let me act in a positive manner
in the way I must to live as I should.
Action is sometimes needed by me.

I am woman, let me be exactly what I am.
Life presents puzzles I must figure out
so I know exactly how I should live.

I am woman, that can be a statement
which is mine to fulfill
because God expects that of me.

Margaret Rahn
Yankton, SD

Defenders of Humanity

For all who defend our nation—
At home and across the sea,
You are an eternal inspiration
To a grateful nation proud and free.

For all who defend our security—
At home and in distant lands,
Our well-being and peace of mind
Reside within your able hands.

For all who defend democracy—
You keep the burning flame alive
Within the hearts of all of us,
Our thirst for freedom you revive.

For all who defend when beckoned—
Wherever duty and bugle call,
We honor service, sacrifice and bravery,
Heads held high and standing tall.

For all who defend around the world
And fight for all humanity,
You make the ultimate sacrifice
For human rights and dignity.

For all who defend our liberties:
We salute you for the hope you give
In defense of peace for all mankind,
Thank you for life we freely live.

Eliza Pleasant McClanahan
Sumter, SC

Eliza Pleasant McClanahan received her bachelor of science degree at South Carolina State University and a master of education degree at the University of South Carolina. In 2008, she retired from teaching after thirty-five years in public education. She is the mother of two daughters, and she and her husband live in Sumter, SC. During her spare time, she enjoys cooking, reading, writing, and researching family history. The poem "Defenders of Humanity" was inspired by the heroic servicemen and women who sacrifice so much to defend our freedoms. This poem is a tribute to them.

Our Path of Life

As we walk down this path of life
There are things we tend to hide
A lot of things we're too busy to see
We never listen to the hum of the bees

Watching the clouds making forms
Seeing the stillness after the storm
The wind whistling through the trees
As the leaves seem to wave to us in the breeze

As the dew glistens on the rose petals
They seem to shine like gold metals
So as you walk down this path of life
Be sure you touch the outstretched hand of a child

Give an elder person you meet a smile
Take a little time to visit for a while
An when our journey down this path ends
We will be together with family and friends

Shirley Winn
Valdese, NC

I am a divorced mother with three children whom I raised by myself. They all grew up and made model parents. I instilled in them the importance of love and helping people. Most people do not stop and listen and feel and see the beauty of the world. They are too busy to enjoy life. This is what inspires me to write. I've always loved people. Strangers are people I haven't met. I'm a happy seventy-five-year-old and give God the thanks for everything in my life. This poem is dedicated to my family.

If Only You Could See

If only you could see
every part of me.
You've hurt me so many times,
I'm almost out of rhymes.

If only you could see
how much you hurt me.
If you can't love me,
then let me be.

Codi Besta
Weaver, AL

Summer

Summer is
very fun,
it feels like it's
never done—
through the
waves of the
ocean blue,
through the
leaves of the
palm trees
green.

Audrey Boyne
Cincinnati, OH

I Met a Child

There are not enough lines in my face
to tell the story of her exquisite grace.

I met a child ...
her twenty-one years etched in her young
form, her heart naïve.
I didn't meet her mind—
perhaps I couldn't reach it.
She waited tables at the local café.
I never knew how much to tip her,
whether it be how hard she tried,
else, a touch of sympathy for the smile
of betrayal in her face, which seemed
to hide a deep bruise. I couldn't afford
her skill.

Strange, how life hurries past us,
yet, seldom we heed. Without a word,
she spoke that summer.

When I asked her name,
"Cathy," she lied,
in deference to an old woman.
I knew I had met an angel.

Carol Chilian
Kerrville, TX

Daddy, Are You Listening?

I'm sitting here next to you on this bench,
telling you about my day and what's been
going on in my life, telling you about your
four great grandchildren, how smart and
beautiful they are.
Thinking back when I was a little girl,
in my eyes you were a big man and my
hero. Daddy, I remember your big soft heart.
You would do anything for anyone, and had a
smile for everyone.
You taught me how to walk and talk,
right and wrong—with Mom's help, of course.
Remember when I put my little hand in yours?
It covered mine like a blanket. I felt safe
and warm.
As the years passed and I grew up, you taught
me so much more. Your hands were soft when
they needed to be, firm when I got into trouble.
A tear falls from my face. Why did
God take you away?
Daddy, thanks for being a great father
and taking good care of me. I miss you and love you.

Janet M. Gerard
Lafayette, IN

His Way

God gives us only what we need,
and not at our own earthly speed.

While trudging on (our only choice),
we close our ears, don't hear His voice.

We grumble, gripe and shed some tears
And long for happy yesteryears.

We see faith dimming, dark as night;
Hope seems to be nowhere in sight.

Then His delay proves our delight;
What seems so hard, He will make light.

We only have to choose to pray
And wait for God to light our way.

Mary Kirnberger
Milwaukee, WI

My Only Dream

My only dream
is that one day
your heart will change
and turn towards my way.

My dream, my love
is when you smile
I'll hear the robins sing
sweet songs of love divine.

My only dream
is when you grieve
the pain will wash away
my tears and dark reprieve.

My only dream is when you dream
that you and I will find and share
the future we'll behold

For me there are no other dreams
...but you alone!

Fidel B. del Rosario
New Britain, CT

Fidel started "scribbling" poetry in his freshman year while training for a poetry-reading contest at St. Vincent de Paul's in Naga City, Philippines. He won second prize reciting Joyce Kilmer's "TREES." He went on to earn his BA in English at St. Bede's College Manila, Philippines. On a scholarship, he went and earned his BA in Spanish at the Instituto de Cultura Hispania Central University of Madrid, Spain. He completed, his graduate studies at the University of Washington in Seattle, WA majoring in romance languages and literature for his master's degree. After briefly teaching bilingual subjects and coworking as a professional chef for more than twenty-five years, he retired four years ago. He now resides in New Britain, CT enjoying his retirement—writing and reading short stories, journals and, of course, poems.

A Tan Line

'Tis the season; time to revel in the rays of the sun, the most beautiful star in the sky.
We all play in it and feel our skin sizzle with its warmth.
But we all must be wary of what comes along with becoming a darker berry ...
the inevitable tan line.
It can be unsightly when it appears; on a shoulder or across the bridge of your nose. Lately, I've been struck by one that I used to have.
Thought it was cute when I saw it everyday, but when I noticed the third finger on my left hand was all one shade, I began to wonder ...
I thought: I didn't need to wear the tan line-causing rings because I didn't want to get them dirty, or I know and he knows we're married, or they needed resizing ...
Then the excuses morphed into, "Whens?"
When was the last time I wore them?
When was the last time I checked in on us and heard something other than an underwhelming response?
When was the last time my child witnessed his parents *in* love?
When was the last time I felt truly appreciated, encouraged and supported?
Then it was easy to remember what happened: those beautiful rings started to become tiny handcuffs, twisting and struggling to cut off circulation ...
Those cuffs transformed, in my mind, into a noose, which got tighter around my neck.
When it's quiet, I can hear the loop and knot scratching against each other, like sandpaper, with my crushed neck as the goal.
I've lost the ability to breathe; I've lost the ability to speak.
I no longer have a voice, nor anything to say, as there is little hope that much will change.
I will, however, muster enough strength and voice to say: "Goodbye."

Kinda France Cooper
Reisterstown, MD

Green-Eyed Monster

Women roll their eyes at me
and deliver me much hate;
they are distant and unfriendly,
afraid I'll steal their mate.

Maybe I don't know I'm pretty
and women's jealousy, which is far from witty,
makes them old in the face,
as they try to make me the disgrace.

They continue to lie on me
as they try and try
to start a new rumor,
which has no humor.

It is me that they wish men
would scorn,
while they who are envious
and forlorn,
get kicked in the ass,
because they have no class.

They have no delight
when their man takes flight,
and they are left alone to simmer and burn
being the recipient of their final spurn.

Lynn Marie Taitt
Baton Rouge, LA

Old Times

You see the times are charging
They're moving too darn fast
Forgetting where they started from
Erasing all the past

You see the times are changing
They feed upon the new
And all the times they followed
Seem lost without a clue

You see the times are changing
They see just what's ahead
The lessons that were paid for
Are buried with the dead

You see the times are changing
They never seem to learn
The best times are behind them
In a place of no return

You see the times are changing
Don't let them fly on by
But learn what they have taught you
And ask the question, "Why?"

Kester Denman
Cotter, AR

I was born in east Texas in the town of Lufkin on July 28, 1946. My grandfather was a judge, my father was a lawyer. I graduated from Stephen F. Austin State University in 1992 with a master's degree in forest and wildlife management. I began to write poetry at an early age and continue to write as of today. This particular poem, "Old Times," was written along with "To Wonder Why?", "Adios," "Wyoming Nights," "Last Phone from La Paz," "Dream Call," "In My Heart," and "I'm Sorry." Thank you for considering my poem in the semi-final round of the National Amateur Poetry Competition.

I Thought of You Today

I thought of you today
And the words that were never said
All the "I miss yous"
And the breaking of the bread.
I thought of you today
And the memories we never got to make
Some of the broken promises
But not all were lost in the break.
I thought of you today
And thought about your laugh
How happy you always sounded
Even if you were sad.
I visited you today
And left flowers on your grave
All I did was shed a tear
because there were no words to say.
I thought of you today
And the holding of our hands
And all I feel are tears
'Cause I know I will never feel them again.

Jackie Clay
Squaw Valley, CA

If I Was a Bird

If I was a bird
I would soar around
I would fly to many places
and I would not be found
I'd be the beauty in the sky
so pretty and majestic
all while looking down
on your world that is so hectic
if I was a bird

Dylan C. Wilson
Kimball, MI

Untitled

Sometimes I wanted to know why I was never loved like everyone
else, Why the light never shined on me.
Why was I left behind forgotten, lost amuse paper.
As if I have no value. With no value what is your worth?
Why are you here who should care?
The clouds still move, the Earth still turns.
The wind still blows. And the grass still grows.
Out of all that the light shines through all the madness.
The light shows what was lost and thought not found is seen.
Hello, no look at me I was always worthy.

Faith Perkins
Rochester, NY

Sally Ann

"Hi Honey! How are you?" That's what she said,
       lovingly, as always,
              when she got *there*—when she met God!

God was surprised—to put it mildly!
       But then—He laughed (yes, He can!)
          and He felt all warm!

You see, He's never had such a loving question addressed to Him,
       Usually it's a plea, once in awhile some "Thanks"
       but *no* one ever asked Him, "How are *You?*"
              (And that "Honey" part?!)

Sally Dietrich
Topeka, KS

She's a Keeper

You worked your way into her life
You charmed your way into her heart
You held her when she was sad
You smiled into her eyes

No one's ever made her laugh the way you have
You said you would never hurt her, you lied
You played with her heart
And toyed with her emotions
You broke her piece by piece

She wasn't smart enough to see what you were doing to her
You said all the right things
And made her feel alive
She was blinded by your charm

You only want her because she's no longer yours
She's a keeper, but you didn't keep her
You did her a favor
And baby that's okay
Because now she's playing your game

Katelyn Horsefield
Oak Grove, MO

A Spiral Golden

Triggers,
And,
Butterfly wings,
Bottled into vacuums,
Beyond death from city light,
A panic room in the dark called existence,
Inside, misfortune just a day forgotten, when carbon-life forms a fossil
	quickly.

Tear it down to the terror design, past the separate dances that
build precious moments, chasing pretty colors to be felt,

A drug running through blood, some superior genetic curve, is far
worse than waking up empty-handed, if some only average sleep
today. Spirit, slice the mystic's eye; fully sober, I curl into dust.

Ringing off from the lips of every wave, every space, that glow
between hourglass sand and her blasted crystal lens; a heavy wake
when counting leaves, or in the sharp call that echoes against every
shell, and in the run of storms with midnight breath.
Living through the motions of a spinning and weaving infinite.

Michael Anthony Kolbash
Tuscon, AZ

My Tears ...

These tears I cry ... are mine. I can't believe you crossed that line.
Never thought I'd see the day, when you'd take your love away.

These tears I cry ... are mine. No, I am not doing fine.
Why did you walk away from me? Was I blind, and did not see?

One day I'll get the truth, since you refuse to tell me now.
What are you afraid of? That I'll hurt you, some way, somehow?

I won't do what you did to me ... can I refuse to let you flee?
No I can't ... because you're gone. Now I know you were a con.

My love for you was true. Given freely, requesting no due.
What did you think that you were missing? While drowning in
nostalgia, reminiscing.

Know this ... it is your loss. My line? You won't get it again to cross.
And my heart? I'll take that back too ... You're undeserving, this much is
true.

I'll be the winner in the end.
My heart will heal and mend.
You've lost your hold, I will be fine ...
Because these tears I cry, are mine.

Melanie T. Koch
Grandview, WA

Dreams Are Forever

When heavy clouds surround you
And there is no light whatever you do
When life seems wasted and hard to take
Can dreams be true or just a fake?

I hate you, childhood dreams, you led me astray
Every moment you fooled me was my bright sunray
You promised me the world and all I desired
Yet, gave me cruel hurdles that left me sad and tired

How can I trust your magic touch today?
Logic says, "Go away"; my spirit begs them to stay
Oh, magic dreams! How can I now ignore?
My mind rejects you, my heart wants you more

A merciful inspiration suddenly appears
It's not for money, glory and fame
It's that promising flame deep down inside
Lightens up the wonders hope can hide

When painful roadblocks make dreams fail
Strength from within will always prevail
Dream, you mortals, of anything but oceans no more
If you cannot lose sight of the shore!

Miranda Athanasula
Silver Spring, MD

Untitled

Sometimes we are truly tested
actions, words that wound
and our feeling of safety is wrested
from our inner womb

Then ensues such a struggle
To look within ourselves
to search for truth during trouble
to prevent our integrity from being shelved

A quest for truth is a must
for both partners in this union
or fall in the ashes of distrust
forever to be coated and burdened

Our energy can be refocused
with honesty, hope and faith
that what we have is our great importance
a gift, a crime to waste

Helen J. Wells
Montpelier, VA

A Word to Describe It

What are the heights,
Where is the quest,
When does a man's soul,
His spirit, know no rest?

Is it a dream,
To never come true,
Or does reality have such a place of
Peace and serenity?

A quiet place to feel inwardly found
and free.

Is there a word to describe it?
Does it glow like a sphere above?

Wait now I think I have it.
Perhaps this thing is called love.

Elaine V. Benson
Antioch, IL

How Great Thou Was and Am

Could I interest you in a story
about a race of people so great,
that the beautiful fragrant flowers bowed
to them as Heaven was their own gate.

A place where people love to be so free
and roses aren't ever just fantasy,
where soldiers do so glorious trails
and birds even talk the news to me.

Who won the stars and stripes forever
in ways the mind would spin,
astronauts rode their silver bullet to the Moon
then rode it back to Earth again.

Songs and music so fair to lift the soul
where stardust fell on Liberty's chin,
airplane pilots sling silverwings across the sky
and dreams unfold, a world of good to win

A place and time when stars were made
this place and Heaven's own so fair,
are all as one and our Father's prayer
wafted like angels on the air.

Where but here on Earth has such all been
and Heaven's all is mixed on in,
and times back then on up to now
make our hearts cry out: we're here again.

Reva L. Kitts
Columbus, OH

I have stood out in the early dawn and watched the pilots sling their planes up and away. I've seen the silver bullets rode by astronauts toward the heavens, and heard and seen the news on TV and radios about the brave soldiers, firefighters, news people, and more, who go to wherever to fight for our freedom. I know who my own family was, and the greatest heroines and heroes that ever were, because of what they've had to bear. The churches, the Kroger store at Graceland here, the people who help us to live anytime... love inspired me.

Virtuous Women

Virtuous women, where does he find?
Help mate soul mate God's second design.
Made for man, out of his side.
Lost in the garden trying to hide.
Embarrassed by her decisions, stuck on her pride.
She forgot about God's original plan:
to stand by his side and support her man.
Don't bash him, criticize him, and knock him down.
Lift him up to wear his crown.
Know her value, know her worth,
know God's purpose for woman on Earth.
A godly woman behind her man.
Her power so strong, can build a land.
But her voice is so loud, she can't hear his plea.
Shhh! Listen, just touch and agree.
The failure is not in him that tries.
The failure is in her that denies
His dreams, his goals, his ambition to strive ...
Let's look at the women from our past lives.
First one up last one down,
doing their part without a frown.
Cooking, cleaning, a listening ear.
Is there anything else I can get for you dear ... ?
See the problem is we hate to submit,
but it's God's message that we don't get.
She should love being the anchor on the boat,
holding it down, keeping it afloat.
You can't see it. It's under the water,
holding strong like no other.
She should be his strength when he is weak,
down on her knees claiming victory.
Every good man has a woman at his side.
Just standing still, allowing him to shine.
Did she play part in his story?
Yes, but a godly woman gives God the glory!

Timeka Walker
St. Petersburg, FL

My Friend

Let me tell you of a man
Who stepped into my life.
In faith he walks in confidence,
"Someday she'll be my wife."

He took me aside and with a smile
He held me in suspense.
He told me of his life and
The things he did repence.

Let me tell you of this man
Who's brought such happiness.
We're equal in that both of us
Has Christ for righteousness.

He brings me special surprises
He tells me of his love.
He promised to take good care of me
And cherishes me as his dove.

Let me tell you of what he did
And what he means to me.
He asked if I would marry him
His bride forever will I be.

He has a way of talking
He tells me how he feels.
He gives me a completeness
And with these rings
Our love it seals.

Sharell Figgins McCleary
Wichita, KS

A Different Me

I sometimes wish I were someone else,
   someone better than me.
A woman who puts all to shame in beauty,
   grace and poise,
A girl who is strong and fleet
   skilled in sport and game.
A woman talented and calm, sure of
   every move,
Maybe a woman who is all of those
   as well as loving, caring, and kind.
I sometimes wonder how it would
   feel to be all this and more,
How it would feel to be someone
   besides just me.

Connie Barker-Allman
Morrow, GA

Freak Out

I hate piles
and piles
of dirty clothes
I hate my brother
screaming
ahh!
I hate being yelled
at a lot
My sister chews with
her mouth open
chum-chum-chum
I hate cleaning
Crash and trash
I hate sushi calling,
"Eat me"

Tamala Stewart
Brooklyn, NY

'Tis the Season

I'm an Xmas tree lightbulb
And my name is One-Two-Three
I lay in a box in the attic all summer long
With no one to sing me as much as one Xmas song
That's all right because we all know
Winter is coming with all that snow
Of course I have all my other bulb friends with me
And we're all waiting anxiously for Xmas season
They shine us up and hook me to new wiring
I'm so happy I should be crying
The tree looks beautiful but the shining glory
Is when the husband says, "Are you ready?"
Here we go One-Two-Three
He flips the switch and low and behold
I'm doing what I was made for
Everyone walking around the tree
Saying how beautiful the ornaments are
My friends and I are shining with glee
I'm an Xmas tree lightbulb
And my name is One-Two-Three
Every time you turn your Xmas tree lights on
You'll remember me

George J. Lamb
Wisconsin Rapids, WI

Let's Start Loving

The ghost of Lincoln walks the corridors
And he paces up and down,
Hoping for a solution
To keep this country from going down.

It's not so easy, he has decided
But he will try to do what's right,
He figures it may take a while
As he paces through the night.

He will call upon his successors
If the solution just won't come,
And he may contact Kennedy
To see what he would have done.

Now he paces and he paces
Until the morning light,
And he may have the answer
If we do it up just right.

We all must pull together
Instead of far apart,
And listen to your neighbor
For he's not so bad at heart.

Instead of killing, let's start loving
And call upon our master from above,
For He will settle everything
And flourish us with love ...

Dorla Fishback
Silver Creek, WA

Teardrops

Sometimes they come when you don't want,
  As days pass by thinking of you,
    And as time passes by—
I hold back many teardrops
  so you can't tell how much
    missing you would be and—
  How much you brighten my days of—
    Only to face holding back the—
      teardrops—I know I should shed.
To help the healing of the pain in missing
                you.
I choke and swallow with sorrow
Just holding back my teardrops forever.
  To await your shoulder, when we meet
                once again
Even though the teardrops do come—
  from time to time when all alone,
    or with the crowd around.
Facing the worry of, Have I done wrong?
  With what you can see, while awatching.
    And listening silently over these teardrops
Then you reply, Don't worry we're together—
  And you've done great—
Then why these teardrops?

Alma Cosner
McHenry, MD

Innocent Casualties

It's been twenty long years in this hellacious addiction
Trapped down here without hope or redemption
It's cost me the price; I said I'd never pay
It had me do things I'd rather not say
Two pieces of my heart lost, this much is true
Trinity and Sierra, Daddy's talking to you
Addiction is strong, someday I pray you understand
I was powerless girls, not even close to a man
Many nights I lay crying, wishing to die
Missing my daughters and asking God why
Why did he take you, so far from me
He should've took my addiction and left us three be
I know it's not easy, accepting God's will
It's only through Him will our hearts ever heal
Addiction has numbed me, but the pain is still there
I've accepted the fact, life's not always fair
I know now the problem which lays inside me
It's the devil's grip of addiction, it's easy to see
Today I declare war on the grip of addiction
Today here with God, I make this my life's long ambition

Mark Blake II
29 Palms, CA

To Minuet

I shall reveal with no regret
That I was born to minuet.
You may dance just as you please
With waggly hips and shaking knees,
With flailing arms and bouncing head,
But from that dance scene I have fled.
No disco and no jitterbug;
No, never will I cut a rug.
I shall repeat with no regret
That I was born to minuet.
I do enjoy a slow pavane,
So stately, dignified and grand.
A dizzying waltz may stir my heart;
Such dancing is indeed an art.
To show one's finery and grace,
One dance alone can set the pace.
So I insist with no regret
That I was born to minuet.
You'll say, "How retro can you get?"
Come hither, friends, and minuet.

Ellen Godfrey
Foxborough, MA

Gardening with Grandson

Grandma take Grandson
  gardening shopping

Grandson gets purple hoe,
  red spade, yellow rake
  green and yellow apron
Grandson pride and joy
  red gloves with little green turtles
Grandma's shopping potting soil
  flowers and green garden gloves

Grandma plants flowers in pots
Grandson plays in the dirt
Grandma waters flowers in the pots
Grandson plays in the mud
Grandma arranges the flower pots
Grandson rides his bike with
  training wheels in his gardening
  outfit and Grandma's
  gardening hat

Mom comes for Grandson
They show Mom his garden
  he planted
Grandma is so proud of
  the garden he planted
Grandma takes pictures
  to show all her friends
Gardening with Grandson

Sallie Heatley
Edmond, OK

*I am lucky to have five grandchildren. The youngest is Gabe, he stays with
me when my daughter is at work. He is slightly autistic so he requires a lot
of attention. We love to garden together. He enjoys showing others his
flowers. He also loves to water his pots of flowers with his duck-shaped
water pitcher. Gabe is so much fun and I am so lucky to be his grandmother.*

The Answer

Jehovah, my God, the great "I AM,"
Before You now I take my stand.
I speak Your name with reverence and love,
I feared You as a child so meek.
Growing older, Your love I did seek.
Creation thunders out your name;
A newborn babe does much the same.
Often I turn to You with all my might,
Seeking answers both day and night.
Why does one beautiful child have to die,
While parents of another child divorce and he cries?
In today's times shootings are common news,
So much sadness makes me sing the blues.
Then I turn to God's love to calm my soul.
Love is the greatest gift or goal.
God gave His son, Jesus, to die for me.
Putting God first, loving God, and loving man,
Will end wars and build trust that all may stand
Humbly in the presence of the great "I AM."

Wanda Carol Turner
Hopkinsville, KY

My name is Wanda Turner, and I live in the blue grass state of Kentucky. I am a wife, mother, grandmother, and great-grandmother. I am a Christian living in a time of violence and a time in which divorce is common. Many people are hurting and seeking a better tomorrow. Sometimes when I am quiet words come to my mind and I am not at peace until I write. That is how I gave birth to this poem and all poems that I write.

Escape

Have you ever wanted to escape
because you just can't possibly relate
to the people you see every day
when you're trying to keep your feelings at bay?

You want to be in a place where you can be you
and not like an animal on display at the zoo
so you put your headphones in
to be sure who you are within.

This is your escape.
It's priceless because it's yours
no one can take that from you
not even if you feel like an
animal on display at the zoo.

Megan Lynn
Danville, PA

Rebirth

A mirror image of me I see yielding to the darkness that
lies within.
Running from the endless possibilities of my dreams,
my soul screams, "Help me please!"

I desire to begin again. I seek newness, revelation,
direction for I've learned to cherish the value in me.

Sweet peace so fills my loins; radiance ignites, the mirror
illuminates for the image of darkness has been captured by
the light.

The newness is me; I've been reborn. The dream to sing, the
fight to exist again has come alive and my endless
possibilities are becoming my realities.

For I have learned to live in the now; you see I am free,
no longer bound!

Chantil M. Dean
Kansas City, MO

Midnight in the Garden of Evil

It's midnight in the garden of evil
Everyone is fast asleep
Here the sorrow has no equal
so you pray the Lord your soul to keep ...
in this nightmare all the while
Strolling through its wilderness deep
lost, aching and quite beguiled
Your soul breaks down and starts to weep ...
Take my hand touch this pain
Hold my heart feel it wretch.
Wrapped in loneliness lost in vain
On my face the sorrow is etched ...
It's midnight in the garden of evil
all around are walking dead.
Here to sit and read the sequel
in Lonely's everlasting bed ...
Your screams for help can't be heard
Destined only to feel her wrath.
Silence swallows every word
In this labyrinth that is the path ...
Dark so thick there is no equal
I'm afraid I've lost my way.
It's midnight in the garden of evil.
So what else is there to say?

Antonio P. Teixeira
Brockton, MA

A Broken Promise

You promised we'd be forever friends,
That you'd hear even my sighs,
But now between us is a border, a fence,
Why did you have to lie?

You promised we would always be together,
You told me we'd walk life side by side.
Do you really understand the meaning of forever?
If you do, then to me you lied.

You promised our friendship-boat would never sink,
That I'd always keep afloat.
But look at me, alone in murky waters,
You're aboard another boat.

But I've cried my last tear; my eyes are now dry,
I'm already moving on.
Let me tell you a secret: you've lost a true gem;
You'll realize, but by then I'll be gone.

Adele Uta
Homer Glen, IL

Haiku for the Birds

I have soared with the chickadee
Fallen headfirst with the nuthatch
I have warmed my hands on the cardinal

Cherie Collett
Benson, VT

You Drain Me

When you come home and are around me, I feel so tense and so blue.
You talk about all things regarding you. My needs and wants take a
backseat while you never miss a beat to personally shine, oh my!

I'm so tired, no fun to be around because you drain me and I'm
so down. Pulling myself up with no help from you. I know I need
emotional support, kindness and understanding and get a clue to stop
suppressing my feelings and allowing you to be so self-absorbing and
cool.

I will work on myself by climbing out of the pit of exhaustion and head
towards the healing light of self love, energy, and fulfillment.

Sharon Gore
Chadbourn, NC

My Deer Pennsylvania

Who made those paw prints impressed
all over the snow so gingerly?
As you casually walk across the snow covered lawn,
what comes into your horn-top head, comfortably
cascading together looking for food non-stop.
The look given as if surprised by a car that
drives up and people stare at your beauty. The
transient stare you give with a tail wagging of
white fluff.
If your viewing is at night flashing headlights guide
you across the street as a signal of safety.
The constant food group picking and all the
while guarding yourselves.
Momma big eyes teaching her young to eat and
be careful among the humans.
Take heart your beauty is always admired each
and every day.
But at last death comes in an instant, for such
beautiful creatures
A sister, brother, mom or a father fall victim to
a cruel hit
My eyes are saddened by the freshly killed furry
victim herewith.
Your recent bony shape starting to
appear without warning
I can take sad comfort that death came quickly
For tomorrow is another day for all
who gather on the grass.
Let's hope your lives are spared for the
remaining furry days
I can see new creatures being born with love

Janet Thevenot
Tobyhanna, PA

Spring

Spring is here, I can tell
The things I see and love so well,
Flowers blooming, birds singing,
Children playing, bells ringing,
This is what spring means to me,
Being lazy, or running free.

Spring is here, the sun is shining,
All through winter we were pining
For sandy beaches, swimming pools,
Climbing hills or using tools,
The garden is the place to be,
When spring is here for you and me.

Spring is here, God's handiwork,
Is everywhere I look;
The mountains and trees, small streams or large seas.
People are merry, their faces cheery.
God is in everything I see,
What joyful blessings for you and me.

Earlene Eastes
Gordonsville, TN

One Fleeting Moment

Come to Mother, precious darling,
Let me cuddle you awhile
Let me feel your baby softness,
Let me see your dimpled smile.

Life is oh, so quick in passing,
Soon you'll be grown and gone from me,
And all these precious things I treasure
Will be just a memory.

So, cuddle closer, baby darling,
Here within my arms, please stay,
That I might drink in all that's precious
Before babyhood doth flee away.

Anna R. Poppleton
Wellsville, UT

Elvis Presley

He was the king of rock and roll.
When he died in 1977 his body was almost stole.
He was born in 1935 and graduated from Humes High.
When he sang his songs the girls would scream and cry.
He made a hit with every song.
When he sang he could do no wrong.
He was drafted in the Army at an early age.
When he did the movie *Jail House Rock* he was in a cage,
He gave all the women a big thrill.
He lived in a mansion on a hill.
To me he was the best singer you could find.
He donated money and was very kind.
He died in 1977 which we recognize this day.
He is still alive, so they say.
He gave to us the music we love.
And he praised God from up above.
He was a religious man in his own right
He learned karate and how to fight.
Elvis died years ago so they say,
but I sure wish he was here today.
Enough about Elvis and more about me.
I'm also a singer and they call me "the king of karaoke"

Terry Russell
Halls, TX

I graduated from the same high school (Humes High) in Memphis in 1967 as the last high school group. I sing now doing karaoke and singing Elvis songs. They call me The King of Karaoke, and Dink (my nickname). I don't do just Elvis. I do everybody's songs like Elvis did but mostly country songs. I have sung at casinos and Memphis clubs and in most of west Tennessee. I am a Vietnam veteran, army and national guard. I am sixty-five years old now, but I still sing karaoke like everyone else, mostly at the VFW in Ripley, TN with friends. I also know George Kline, one of Elvis's good friends. He works at Horseshoe Casino.

Smile

Like a house without
doorways like a yard with
a flower, like a clock without
a main spring that
will never tell the hour.

A thing that makes you
so sad his a face
without a smile it
will lose the cost to
care and ease the ways
of sins. This will help
you on the longest road
a cheer you might by a mile.
and so whatever is your
lot, just smile, and smile,
 and smile.

Flavilee Gizene
Cape Coral, FL

*I was born in Jamaica West Indies. My parents were Anetta and Rubert
Morrison. I was one of nine children. I was the seventh child. I was born
into a Christian home. My father, Rubert, was a tax collector and my mother,
Anetta, a seamstress. I was a very happy child but I always wanted to be a
singer. So I started singing in the choir of the England Church on the Chiox
in Jamaica, and when I embarked to the United States of American in late
1979, I'd had my citizenship for over twenty years. I have worked in the
medical field for twenty-seven years and to this day I am still singing in the
choir. But as a child I just knew I was born for something special. I would
just stand there making up little songs and saying little poems without being
taught to say it.*

The Message

Are you in control of your life
Or is someone controlling you
If so let the message your guide be
For the message does not change
But faithful and true remains
It however can change your life
Put you in control
It can give you hope and a faith strong and sure
For the love of God transcends all things
So give your life to God and believe
For His message brings new beginnings
Thus start over and take control
Come to know God's kingdom is real
Not a feeling felt in the heart
But 'tis a true heartfelt feeling to sustain and help you
So study this message that does not change
Sound it deep in your heart and feel its power
Know that you can call to God at any hour
Let the message change your life
Stand up! Take control
Be counted a friend of God
Whose heart is eternal and whole
His son's life was given for you
Can you do less than follow through

Lillian Merrell
Battle Creek, MI

Who I Am

I am the blue sky.
The sun rising in the morning.
I am waterfalls in a valley.
The soothing sound of water hitting rocks.
I am the smell of blooming flowers.
I am wet dew on the grass in the morning.
I am the feel of a cool breeze on your face.
I am the love people feel for others.

Ciarra Morse
Buchaman, GA

I have blue eyes and brownish hair. My favorite color is pink. I like to watch TV. I love to go swimming with my big brother, and I love animals, especially dogs. I love to roller skate. I have five dogs and love them all. My favorite show is Sam and Cat.

My Room Is Alive

My windows open with a spark of surprise
Which causes my covers to arise
And for I go into shock

Clothes making a dive
With moving eyes; alive
I'm on a mission

Tennis racket in one hand
I make a ferocious stand
And I'm ready to attack

Fists clenching
Stare fixing
And I make a swing for the clothes

The clothes purr
The pillows run with a blur
And I come up with a conclusion

My room isn't alive!

Tails peek from shirts
And whiskers appear
Making me lose my fear

No evil omens
No bad luck

Time to go to bed

Socks move and
Shoes growl

Uh Oh!

Meghan Merritt
Hillsborough, NC

Lighthouse

Waves of desperation had almost consumed my peace, joy and life.
I began to sink into a sea of sorrow, as the currents of
disappointments began to overtake my spirit. Although my lips
couldn't pray, the spirit in me moaned for the living God my
Redeemer. When the shell of me became lifeless and my heart beat
became faint, the Father rescued me. The Father blew the breath of
life back into my spirit and nourished me with His fulfilling words.
Quick, powerful, sharper than any two-edged sword, did He slice and
destroy the yokes of bondage. I was made whole; I was set free
indeed. I realized every storm I weathered He allowed, for the
making of me. Every time waves attempt to wash me off the shore,
I cleave to the rock who is my strong tower. I survived to lead
others to the island of refuge, for He rescues all those that call on His
name, Jehovah. When the land around us seems dark and desolate,
He stands as a lighthouse letting us know help is on the way.

Yvonne McChristian
Mernillville, IN

Hidden Secrets

When you think of odd,
What do you think of?
What are secrets to you?
Well maybe secrets are odd, unique, strange or weird.
Weird is a book that cannot be read.
Unique is a blanket without any thread.
Odd is a crayon without any color.
Or maybe if you sum it all up,
It's life.
The life we live in, the life we treasure,
The life we travel through, the life we know.
So, think again, if you think someone else is weird, odd, or different.
Because we all know everyone has a hidden secret in their life.
It may be bills, a love of mice, a craving for pickles and ice cream.
Maybe your secret doesn't show.
Maybe no one will ever know.
So what do you think is strange?
Your home, your town, your city, your state, your country, your
continent,
Or is it the world you live in?
Maybe the strangest thing is right under your nose,
Maybe it's your life.
You can't hide from it,
You can't run, you can't turn back on it.
Somehow, someway
Your life will always encounter strange secrets.

Wyatt Wichman
Watertown, WI

The Perfect Rose

The perfect rose is pastel peach.
Its petals hold the dew.
The vines climb upward, out of reach
but still within your view.

The stem is strong and holds each rose
up to the morning sun.
The thorns protect it as it grows,
for it's the fairest one.

The leaves are there to catch the rain.
They never miss a drop.
The perfect rose can be quite vain ...
expecting clouds to stop.

The rose is quite magnificent.
Its fragrance has a power.
I can't recall another scent
which lingers like this flower.

Aroma like a spring bouquet.
Its petals never close.
Just briefly winter steals away
this deeply rooted rose.

Rosebuds begin to sprout in spring ...
thirsty for April showers.
The blooms beneath the monarch's wings
become the perfect flowers!

Ann Boyle
Kennewick, WA

My Shae Shae

The day we first met
She was scared and a shaky mess
I took her to the vet
She calmed down no more no less
Her nails were long and curled
She ate and began to hurl
Her teeth were yellow and stained
She did not want to be trained
Her face was filled with despair
She had eyes that were unaware
Her hair was unkempt and shedding
She had a bath, and laid on her bedding
Her walk was slow and unsteady
She could not bark, she was not ready
Her head was lowered with sadness
But before long, she was proud with gladness
She began to run, jump and play
Her demeanor had changed every day
She was rescued from her fate
Her life now is glorious and great
She is loved and treated well
Now, she is happy and out of her shell
She guards the house like it's a mansion
Because her life is full of expansion
She is my wonderful companion
She is my Shae Shae, home at last.

Faye Cephus
Marlin, TX

Summer

The bright summer sun shines on down
No one could ever have a frown

There's a breeze coming from the west
This season has to be the very best

The grass is as green as sugar snap peas
The sun is as golden as bumble bees

The fresh dew is as cool as a morning breeze
The pollen in the air seems to make me wheeze

The clouds gently float on by
The humidity is thick in the sky

The lake is shimmering like glitter
While this land is teaming with critters

Nothing compares to this season
There's no need to give a reason

Sarah Lemke
Oak Grove, MN

Rainbows

Rainbows, rainbows
Rainbows here, rainbows there
Rainbows everywhere.

Rainbows, rainbows,
Rainbows left, rainbows right
I wish I could see a rainbow at night.

Rainbows, rainbows
Rainbows fade, rainbows glow
Rainbows I love you so!

Mary Feagle
Jasper, FL

Hope

Facing the same fears
Wiping the same tears
I turn my life around
My feet firm on the ground
I feel hope by my side
Knowing that will be my guide
No one more to hold me back
Trust in myself I no longer lack
I find my way out
The dark tunnel of doubt

Carolyn Tomlinson
Burbank, CA

Untitled

Please give me
your unbraided pulse
in a bible, your blue knees
in a cracking jar
a morning from that year of blinks
all of your creases, any
of our sighs
plant these things in the crooks of my arms
under the curl of my hair
sing them to sleep, pray them
out of bonelessness.
I want the violet of your throat scattered in my hands,
your star-stuff, your bruised breath, your loneliness.
buried under last year's tan
growing, growing
until I can feel your origami heart,
thin with wanting
not to want this.

Kira Tsougarakis
Englewood, NJ

Pier 14

Pier 14, better than 12 or 13.
Pier 14, not as good as 15 or 16.
Pier 14 is where I stand to meet my fate,
thus, where cold, aggressive actions will happen tonight.
I hope I'm not too late.
I hope my soul doesn't take flight,
I will set the trap and bring the bait,
I will justify my actions, making them right.
Tonight is the night, I can no longer wait.
Pier 14 is where the truth will be told,
after this night, no more worries, no more tripe.
I won't let this problem haunt me as I grow old,
it will all become clear on this pier tonight.
Cowards, they stay home, and rest their hands and feet,
but I will rise and put down my enemy's so-called plight.
Pier 14 is where I will be,
Pier 14 is where I will have bolder sight
than my enemy, whom I will vanquish out to sea.
I will move forward with a powerful might,
against numerous odds, many there will be.
Fighting back a raging current I call my life,
outmaneuvering giant obstacles, trying to swim upstream.
There will be blood; there will be gunpowder, a courageous fight.
When the time arrives, I shall strike!
After the battle concludes, I shall walk away, unharmed and alive,
for Pier 14 will be my Great Savior tonight!

Jake Wasinger
St. Charles, IL

Grandmother's Table

Wooden square
Heavy impressive legs
Marked with years of wear
But not abused
Countless meals sat upon it
Faint echoes of conversations linger
Aged
At long last abandoned
Broken down, lopsided
Slightly warped
Rescued with visions of nostalgia
Downsized to a coffee table
Stately placed
In another age
Oncoming memories
Will keep it alive
My grandmother's table

Julia Gonzales
Salt Lake City, UT

To Jill

The old man looks at what once was
And in the furnace of his mind
Reheats the ash of memory,
His cold dead pleasure to re-find.

The young man dreams of what will be
And builds his stairway to a star,
Stacking hope up loftily
For pleasure twinkling from afar.

But I live in the here and now,
And hold my pleasure in my arms;
Enough for me that I should love
And be the arbor for her charms.

Edward D. Carpenter Jr.
N. Huntingdon, PA

This poem was inspired by the love of my life. True love doesn't seem smooth. We separated and after fifty years found one another. And so it was in the butterfly garden of the Norwin Public Library, surrounded by friends and witnessed by a young minister who started life as a carpenter, we were joined as one. Expanding joy and incredible blessing deeded by God as destination of the future. Every day has been a perfect blessing.

The Sign on the Wall

The sign sly-winking 24 HR ATM
hints at a withdrawal,
and beyond it all,
there's a crack in the wall
and the building is leaning
on a small tree.
If I don't make a deposit today
the bank will fall.

Kimie Gill
Sierra Vista, AZ

I've been blessed to have lived for many years in places like Japan and Hawaii. I now look out my window at one of Arizona's most awesome mountain ranges. I'm an environmental advocate and a social progressive at heart. Nature offers inspiration and my progressive leanings occasionally peek out from my poems. But life in all its varying shades, moods, voices, and nuances is what really moves me. I hope to keep writing poetry till I've breathed my last. The talk about banks is so dismal—a little whimsy to lighten things up a bit.

Till You Come Back

I'll be waiting, here at home
I'll keep watching, all alone
I'll be listening for the phone
the time, it passes, oh, so slow
Until the day you've come back to me
I'll be waiting, patiently
You're all that matters
You're my whole world
I pray each day to God above
That he sends you back to me, my love
You're all that matters
You're my whole world
You make me proud, to be your girl
You're my hero, you see
Because you're out there in the fight
We all sleep better, here at night
The stars and stripes, flying free, above
Because of you, my love
Seems like an eternity
Since you've been gone
But I'll do my best, to carry on
I'll see you in my dreams, tonight
Till you come back, and hold me tight
Sweet dreams and good night.

Gwendolyn V. Nickolson
Pueblo, CO

I grew up in the Maryland suburbs of Washington, D.C. and was a teenager of the radical '60s. My favorite teacher, Mr. Henderson, was killed in Vietnam, five months after he left the classroom. My friends that came back from Vietnam had problems, including PTSD. Dad, a WWII vet, had many of the same problems. He spent the last six years of life in a V.A. Hospital. When I went to visit, I'd see all those vets with missing limbs and spinal cord injuries. It broke my heart. This is to honor all war vets, past and present.

Ode to Aging

As a young man in my prime,
A stronger body you could not find.
My bulging muscles I could flare
And throw my body in the air.
I'd twist and turn—jump and bend,
On exercise I could depend
To keep my body in a mend.
But time has taken its heavy toll
Upon my body and my soul.
For when I try to perform
The leaps and jumps that once were norm
This aching body tells me true,
This is not what I now can do.
Where rippling muscles used to be,
Just sagging skin is all you see.
Don't feel bad, I have been told,
That's how it is when you grow old.

Joan R. Jones
Cudahy, WI

Untitled

The sparkle in your eye,
The warmth of your skin.
Your breath on my neck,
That shakes me within.

The touch of your hand,
The smell of your hair.
The naughtiness in your smile,
That strength in your stare.

Your kiss on my lips,
Your body near mine.
The stroke of your touch,
That feeling inside.

The compassion in your embrace.
The power in your face.
The beating of your heart.
That we may never part.

The beauty of your kiss,
And that magic in your touch.
It is for all these reasons and more,
Why I love you so much ...

Jacob Sanger
Ft. Mohave, AZ

The Feast

Parched and hungry come,
Enter the Lord's banquet hall,
Craving cooling water,
And sustenance that is palatal.
Seated, His smile invites.
See and taste the goodness.
The abundance of the ages fills,
The eyes with a refreshing spectacle.
Living water spills
Forth from the fountain of life,
For arid and withered souls to drink
In the coolness and be revived.
Spread out in copious amounts,
Succulent fruits for one's essence.
Platters filled with joy, goodness and peace.
So pleasing to the taste.
Let the heart marinate in His mercy
And grace until it is tender.
Soak in the flavor of His love.
Dredge the mind in His every
Promise to be satisfied through and through.
His compassion crimps the rough edges of life,
Sealing out cares of this world.
Each word coated by His blood.
Feast at His table for abundant life awaits.

Kathleen Will
Coldwater, MI

A New Life

I have so much to be thankful for
God blesses me everyday,
And all I really have to do
Is open my heart and pray.

He has filled my life with joy
Gave me a reason to sing,
My life is not the same now
I've given Him everything.

I let Him take my pain and heartache
He has my every care,
And when my spirit needs a lift
I'm lifted up through prayer.

He sacrificed His only son
So my soul would not be lost,
My past was all wiped away
When they nailed Him to the cross.

He died knowing me
And that I would be full of sin,
But He arose from the grave
So I could be born again.

I walk a different road today
Since I opened my heart's door,
I heard Him knock, I let Him in
And I will serve Him forever more.

Sylvie Cyr
Ellington, CT

I am a born again Christian, my poems seem to come from the Lord when I'm in prayer and feel his presence the words just flow, I don't have to think of the next line or verse. I just write the words down. I have over eighty religious poems, one day I would like to publish them in one book. I'm sure there is one or more that would touch the reader's heart.

Eulogy for a Dog

He was bold and proud, his presence fierce,
With love, your heart he would pierce.
A faithful heart, with me he'd run,
Wind-blown coat, thirst for fun.
Dark of night, he would stay
To guard my soul where I lay.
Keep me from harm and death's dark maw.
A gentle lick, a comforting paw
With devotion, never to ask
Never to wane, or shirk a task.
Roads of freedom, we would ride
My faithful dog at my side.
Gone now, but I still see
How he pressed my side, head on my knee.
Stories untold, no time to tell
Goodbye my pet, hail and farewell.
We'll meet again at Heaven's gate.
I promise you, I won't be late.
All shall pass, kingdom come.
Once gain, with you I'll run.

James A. Chapman
Greensburg, IN

Jim lives in Greensburg, a small town in southern Indiana. A lover of dogs having raised chow chow's for twenty years, he enjoys nature and history of all sorts.

A Ride to Freedom

I was richly blessed with a wonderful life,
Two children, grandchildren, and you my wife.
Great times we had in our forty-five years,
Then the time came when we faced our fears.
My mind was filled with knowledge, so active and clear,
And then it got muddled with Alzheimer's, I hear.
I gave it my best, and you know I tried,
But night after night I lie there and cried.
I was no longer the man God intended me to be,
And I could not bear having loved-ones take care of me.
How embarrassing that was to a strong man like me,
Oh thank God I am now free!
I loved my cycle as you well know,
So I jumped on it and decided to go.
Lightning flashed and thunder roared,
The wind blew and the rain poured.
I kept riding that cycle of silver chrome,
When all at once, God called me home.
The pain has now left, and my mind is clear,
The pressure has been lifted from me my dear.
Please don't be mad because I took that last ride,
Just know angels went with me and flew by my side.
I heard glorious singing in beautiful tone,
Then I saw our Lord, and guess what, He is on a throne!
I have the wind in my hair and a smile on my face,
Oh what freedom in this beautiful place.

JoAnn Howell
Prague, OK

Don't Give Up!

When "yes" is in your future
Don't worry about the "nos."
God will grant your heart's desire
In the midst of all your woes.

You might feel defeated,
Like you've done all that you can.
Though the "nos" seem almost endless,
Try it once again.

When Elijah asked for rain,
Six times the Lord said, "No."
The seventh time one tiny cloud
Brought God's grace to all below.

The "nos" are just a test.
Do you believe what God can do?
If he placed the desire inside your heart,
Do you trust He'll see it through?

Though you may suffer setbacks,
And just can't achieve success,
The very next attempt you make
Might be when God says, "Yes!"

Debra D. Hess
Concordia, MO

Voice of Grief

He did not wake today to die,
And yet he did, left questions: why?
The pills he took put fear aside
Were not the kind he was prescribed,
No way, he would have known the toll,
Because he thought he had control.
But chemicals deceived his mind,
Rejected hands the helping kind,
His heart pumped past its normal beats,
And stressed the body's natural streets,
Cruel silence fell upon the scene,
His fallen life and ended dream,
Addiction-death was not his choice,
Our grief is now his only voice!

Robert Lee Larson
Dayton, NV

Soul Weeds

The dry ground has seen some rain.
"Sing praises for the rain!"
The weeds in my garden will weep
As I pull them out by their roots.
Some flowers are still asleep.

Shortly, new weeds will take their place
And once again I will frown and complain.
Then fiercely I will work the soil.
Some flowers will bloom in full array.
They ignore my endless toil.

Today I feel another garden
One that only God can see.
It, too, seems full of many weeds.
God beckons me to keep it clean
When Satan plants his ugly seeds.

I wonder how often His living water
Has traveled through my veins.
He is sad to see weeds, where there were none.
Oh, yes, He knows each garden well,
The seeds of sin in every one.

What a heavy price He paid,
Sacrificing His only son.
I have soul weeds, as He can see.
Before their roots grow deep
Send living water to set them free.

Janice E. Mansfield
Angola, IN

Untitled

I have been told a story of a very little girl
who climbed a windmill to its very top
and felt the breeze flow through her hair and flip a curl.
How exciting it is to reach the next step and stop
to look up and to view the surrounding world.

Then to see it's a very long way to the ground,
she is like a little kitten—where to now?
And to hear a falling stone make a frightful sound.
Gently she is rescued by a familiar strong right hand,
but to reach great heights it's better to look up, not down.

Jerry Sharp
West Des Moines, IA

Untitled

To me, you are the only one
  My heart belongs to you
I'll love you every day of my life
  And ever after too.

Some day that special "I do" vow
  Will join us man and wife
Together we'll share our joys and sorrows
  As one throughout our lives.

Janet M. Dias
Manteca, CA

The Wonder of Wind Chimes

How the wind must love to orchestrate
Those gentle wisps of sound.
We have no way to contemplate
what note will next resound.

The mood of the wind sets the mood of the chime,
Unpredictable sounds that you cannot mime.
They may be as soft as an angel's kiss,
That will enter you into a state of bliss.
Yet other times, as the wind grows bold,
An uproarious mixture of sounds unfold.

They almost appear to be singing at times,
'Tis the wind's expression through the movement of chimes.
So enjoy all the sounds that the chimes do bring,
From the gentle in summer to audacious in spring.
Their sound is most pleasing for all to hear,
And they play their sonata all through the year.

Shirley Buckley
Hemet, CA

Hear Me Ye Men and Women of a Dead World

Hear me ye men and women of a dead world of how it used to be.
Ye had a world of great value in the eyes of all.
You lived in peace but sometimes there would be a small war between
    a free and a non-free country.
But these weren't bad, only a few thousand would die, or maybe more.
There were three giant nations on the planet of yours.
There were two bad and one good, or were they all bad?
They would fight one another all the time.
One would try to take a small country and another would try to stop
    them.
One day one of these nations launched a rocket into space.
It didn't make it and almost blew up one of these nations.
They talked of peace so that this world could go on living and not die
    out.
This peace lasted for about fourteen years before these nations wanted
    more.
Then it happened, the one thing that these nations didn't want, but got.
It was called the atomic war, or world war three.
It left this world bare and it had no life upon it.
This was once a great planet, but now there is no life upon it.
This was the third planet in the Milky Way galaxy, or it was once called
    Earth.

Timothy H. Johnstone
Porterville, CA

Nesting

The kids are grown,
The kids are gone
So is the nurturing need
Strange indeed
Roots and wings
Still so many things
But just in case
We remain home-base
To listen and to share
To love and to care
I love my wife
Still so much to life

Rick Calvelli
Cedarburg, WI

Valentine's Poem

Granddaddy, I know that you're not here anymore and I
know you know too, but you're in a better place now and I
will always love you. You have been through your tough life,
you were a special man and I know Grandma was happy to
be your wife. January ninth was a sad and depressing day but
at the end I knew it was going to be okay. I loved you since
birth but now I have to let you go. I knew you weren't ready
but that's just how life flows.

Cameron Kirby
Dale City, VA

Sacrifice

Early in the morning
Late at night
You were willing
To serve and fight
For this *great* nation
And all that is right
You were willing
To serve and fight

Stories we have heard
Lives we have shared
Thank you
For all you have
Bared

May we take this moment
Just to say
To each man and woman
And their families
Who gave
More than we
Ever knew
Thank you, thank you, thank you
For the
Red, white and blue

Lora C. Stone
Lumberton, NC

Obtuse

Loving someone, anyone,
Everyone is hard work.

No one, nobody,
Alone
No man
No woman
No child

God is love.
And I—me and you?
We are ... what?

Children, babies
Human beings.
Creatures ... who?

Is it deliberate?

Kim Parsons
Ravenswood, WV

World Trade Center: An American Tragedy

On September 11, 2001, thousands of Americans were injured and many lives were taken away by a group of thoughtless, heartless terrorists committing an atrocious act of murder on this day.

America has always been the home of the brave and the land of the free, and this murderous act of terrorism will not change the way we act or what we can say.

These murderous terrorists have destroyed our beautiful buildings and taken many innocent lives with this horrendous act.

But with our love of God, our love of each other, and our love for a free America, we will always keep coming back.

My thoughts and prayers are with those who lost their loved-ones, and those that were injured too.

And during your time of mourning for lost loved-ones, all Americans and the world will be mourning with you.

My prayers and thanks to the thousands of volunteers who worked so relentlessly and refused to stop.

The strength and determination again shows all the world that America stands united and will always be on top.

Bob Tarvin
Dadeville, AL

Mother and Son

My nineteen year old son, home on a brief leave from the Army,
is deploying shortly to Afghanistan for the first time.
My mind is not wrapping around this well;
my thoughts are scattered and all I can think, over and over,
is that he is going away to this foreign place and I have
no magic in my mother's medicine bag to keep him safe.
I don't share this with him, but for the next nine months
my overnight bag will be packed with my passport,
ready for travel at a moment's notice if needed—
an emotionally fragile way to live.
He is not my easiest child; always independent
and determined to walk his own path,
and I acknowledge that I cannot walk this one with him,
although no doubt my imagination will.
In moments of weakness I confess I have prayed
that time would stand still and hold us all in safe frozen poses.
At this stage in his life he cannot really understand
how incredibly, desperately dear he is to me.
While we are talking, I smile for his sake and swallow my unspoken fears.
Looking across the table, I have one of those flashes of sudden
     recognition—
with startled pleasure I see that his eyes looking back at me are my eyes;
level blue-grey eyes just like mine and so much more mature
than you would expect to see looking out from such a young face.
He is talking but I am not hearing words;
I am watching how the light is already changing
the planes and angles of his beloved face and all I can think is,
"Please God, just keep him safe."
We have finally gotten past those prerequisite years of painful
teenage skirmishes and are beginning to really understand each other;
I am so very proud of the person looking back at me and I cannot lose
     him now.

Cindy Pirson
Buffalo, NY

The Mind that Wished to Be

I live within my mind, and sometimes I think I'm fine.
I look at the world around me, and wish I could define what defines a
    normal mind.
Sometimes I am happy, sad, laugh, and feel I am part of the world.
Other times,
I ask who this is within my mind who speaks so loud and clear,
And tells me things I do not want to hear.
I wonder if others hear these voices that torment me in-between my
    happy times.
And then I am told, this is life for only a certain few who are what we
    call the mentally ill.
Oh, the awful pain it brings to be defined of such a name.
Lies, lies you see, for I hear them you must believe.
Sometimes I see them tormenting me!
How can you say this is not real to me?
Oh the awful dread I feel, when I am told I am mentally ill.
The voices come and go, and you have to fight them off as you go day
    by day.
Until one day, you finally say,
I had enough and cannot stay.
I must go to a quiet place.

Eliezer Stalowski
Greendale, WI

A Piece of Peace

Speaking the word "peace" seems to create soothing within the soul.
As I swing on my patio swing, its essence yearns to take a toll.
The early morning sunshine melts my being as I glide to and fro.
Nothing seems to matter except my inner calm which opts to grow and
      grow!

This rare tranquil moment beckons a comfort within me like none other
      has.
Oh, how I wish I could salvage it forever, never allowing it to pass.
Feeling this flowing peace inspires me to be still.
All my surroundings seem frozen in time—the aura is incredibly surreal!

Within the quiet, nature invites me to listen to each sound that is near.
God's artwork unfolds and whispers silence loud and clear
Now realizing this defining moment in time will no longer be.
Patience assures me that another future piece of peace
will graciously offer itself to me ...

Dawn Killmer
Bella Vista, AR

Take the Time to Look Up in the Beautiful Sky

Take the time to look up in the beautiful sky
Sometimes cloudy a mass of vapor,
Rain condensed water falling in drops from the sky
Take the time to look up in the beautiful sky

Hail—frozen rain in small balls
Rainbow—colored arch of sunlight-rays through raindrops
Snow—precipitation frozen in crystal flakes
Take the time to look up in the beautiful sky

Sun—star-rays of the solar system
Stars—heavenly body of radiating light
Take the time to look up in the beautiful sky

Moon—satellite of the Earth
Take the time to look up in the beautiful sky
Looking low all the time you miss all the
Beauty of God's handiwork and won't
Appreciate His beauty of holding your
Head up sometime in the sky

Josie Loche
Bastrop, LA

My name is Josie Benton Loche. My parents are Mr. Felton and Dora Benton. I was married to the late Milous Loche, and I have ten children and extended family. I was raised by grandparents Mr. and Mrs Winfield Benton from the age of two, who taught me you can do whatever you are inspired to do by acknowledging God first. My grandparent made sure I got an education, high school and then college. Education, wisdom, and inspiration from God gave me the idea to write the poem. I attend a Bible teaching church called New Light. The pastor, Reverend J. Green, is an inspiration for us to believe you can do anything if you try.

Flowers

Flowers can be sent
for love that never ends
or for a love for friendship of a friend.
They can be sent for a cover-up
what you intend
to control your loved-one's life
or a friend.
There are many ways to send
flowers, to a loved one or a friend;
let's hope it's for love
and not what you intend
for God knows all things
and will control the end.

Marie Malone
South Point, OH

Dreams—Surreal

I sometimes see visions
of things that aren't there.
My eyes are closed—
but it seems that I stare.

I say I don't believe
in ghosts of the night.
But they seem surreal
I sometimes think—I might.

I reach for the light
but the light isn't there.
I stumble in the darkness
Then—I fall down the stairs.

Robert Campbell
Sarasota, FL

My wife tells me I have nightmare dreams. She shakes me to wake me up. A while back, the hard tile floor woke me up. Next morning with blood on the bed sheets, I wrote this story "Dreams Surreal."

Gone, but Not Forgotten

When your heart is breaking,
And the loss is hard to bear,
Whisper a prayer, to the Savior,
And your heavy load, He'll share.

Find a smile in the sunshine,
And a kiss amongst the dew;
You'll find, your heart is lighter,
And comfort will come to you.

Take a moment to remember,
Things you and your loved one did;
So search those photo albums,
Their faces are *not* hid.

There's peace and comfort waiting,
They're alive, within your heart;
They may be gone in body,
But their memories, did not part.

Go to your favorite places,
Make time, in your busy day;
All in all, you'll feel better,
And take some time, to pray.

They're gone but not forgotten,
Your love is still very strong;
Cherish all those days together,
And your heart will find a song.

Carole Vance
Minot, ND

A Hidden Vale!

Have you heard about the good samaritan,
Down in a cute little rabbit hole?
Well, down in a hidden valley,
Behind an industrial complex,
Behind a Ford dealership and Slumberland.
We slumber and live in our home
In the Valley, out of public view.
Our diner is a drive-in restaurant,
And most of us do drive in
Wheel chairs, no less!
We eat and sleep, play Bingo,
And attend church services;
There are brain teaser games,
Card games, and fun things to draw.
We do not need public scrutiny,
We have it all, here with the
Bunnies and squirrels for
Entertainment.
Bird feeders at every bedroom window
Attract cardinals, a downy woodpecker,
Black-cap chickadees, sparrows,
And other birds.
It's quiet and peaceful
Here in God's little valley, good Sam
No less!

Lorrian Wentz
Inver Grove, MN

For My Brian

Do you believe in love?
Love at first sight?
I sure do.
And it was so right!

He's tall, dark, and handsome,
Good-looking as he can be.
But when I first saw him,
He was a wee baby.

When I first fell in love,
He was six weeks old and sound asleep
In the caseworker's car
In a baby seat.

We had prayed for a child.
God led us to adoption.
He knew it would be
A wonderful option.

I loved that baby at first sight
As all mothers do
And to this day and forever
I'll tell him, "I love you!"

Marsha Davis
Silver Lake, IN

Patience

When but a child I had goals
To make come true before growing old
I was free to be happy and plan you see
For there were others responsible for me
I knew nothing at all about patience

I knew not that my mother wept
Not the toils and tears and pain she felt
She loved me so she made a shield
So that pain and anguish I would not feel
So patience was not profound to me

It takes time and some misery to know
How years of heartaches can make you grow
You learn to pray and keep the faith
The time finally comes when you say, "I will wait"
That is when you begin to learn patience

When all your problems get so great
That you say, "No more can I take"
You pray so hard and so very long
But it seems like everything goes wrong
Hold on with patience and hum a song

God will come like a mist of rain
He will wash away all grief and pain
He will leave so quiet and so smooth
You won't know when he entered or left the room
Trusting in the Lord will make you patient

Carrie E. Bridges
Huntsville, AL

Untitled

I set My bow in the cloud,
The sign of unfailing promise.
Look up to the Heavens and give Him glory,
He who is ever true.

I give My commandments to you,
The sign of unfailing justice.
Look up to the Heavens and give Him glory,
He who is ever true.

I set My son on the cross,
The sign of eternal salvation.
Look up to the Heavens and give Him glory,
He who is ever true.

Oh risen son of God,
The sign of forgiveness and mercy.
Look up to the Heavens and give Him glory,
He who died for you!

Martha Gunderson
Goodland, KS

It's Your Birthday

Today it's your birthday and we're all glad that it's here.
If it wasn't for God you would not be here
So we will all praise God
With the greatest of love
Because we now have you to love

Nathan Hand
Independence, MO

God Took the "Want To" Out of Me

Go on down that dusty road, with your
friends and a heavy load, as for me
I'll stay right here, with my new friend
that is near. For God took the "want to"
out of me.
Once I too was just like you. I could
party the whole night through
Now, God has taken the "want to" out of me
made everything brand-new
He would be a friend to you if you
would only ask Him to. Then God would
take the "want to" out of you, like He
took the "want to" out of me.

Lelia E. Haddox
Weirton, WV

If I Didn't

If I didn't seek the Lord,
And He never found me,
Where would I be today?

If I never prayed to the Lord,
And He never answered me,
Where would I be today?

I prayed to the Lord,
"Lord please heal me,"
And He answered my plea.
Now, I know where I'll be.

I thanked the Lord
And will always thank Him
And I'll be close to Him
For there is where I want to be.

Thanking Him
  Thanking Him.

Palmyra Benjamin
St. Croix, US Virgin Islands

Why Me?

Why me? I asked you Lord
When placed upon your list.
Aren't there others more deserving
To ascend into your midst?

There are many better suited
I'm sure you must agree
Of leading people by the hand
To salvation's walk with Thee.

Why me? I asked again
For talents I have none,
And being devoted completely to you
I've only just begun.

You answered me quite clearly:
I've watched as you grew
It's faith that brought you here to me
And that faith will see you through.

The mistakes you'll make are many,
The successes just a few,
But your heart remains focused all on me,
And that's why I chose you.

Albert H. Moore
Santa Fe, TX

Wisdom

She left
as she was being ignored

She left
as anarchy lifted its sword

She left
as everything turned from the right

She left
as good gave up its fight

She left
as they all applauded decay

She left
as they turned and went their own way

She left
as the fabric of decency was torn

She left
as the children of folly were born

She left
as the fear of God was no more

She left
as she wrote "Ichabod" over the door

Larry Redding
Graham, NC

Love Can Be Found at Midnight

At midnight underneath the moonlight. I have found my true love. His eyes are the color of the noon sky, that I wish to fly high in a plane someday. Where it's going to take me to London's bridge and back to America, where the land is free. His skin feels like feathers rubbing all over my flesh. Until I become the snow that melts on the ground. My eyes burn with desire. While I look into his and see flames going higher. When morning comes I go outside. I look around me the trees are blowing while the birds are singing a happy song. I get in my car and I drive with not a care in the world. Because my soul is dancing. But when I get on main street. I visit the one that gave birth to me in the fall. Where some leaves turn red. Like my face did, when she yelled at me. Until she got blue in the face. Because she found out that I had discovered a love that was more beautiful than any ocean that I have dreamed of seeing. My heart said forever on it and his was saying the same thing. After that scene had happened that day, I looked back and I had started a war that I would have to fight and win at the end. She can't kill our love, it's the only thing that is alive and bleeding our name. Age is just a number. So are the years. I'll be spending with my rose. I go to the riverbank and watch the water run, I visualize us and a two-story house with horses and the pasture roaming. When nighttime comes you'll find us outside on the balcony. Where our love can be found at midnight underneath the moonlight.

Kenya Jarrell
Adairsville, GA

I Feel So Lonely

I feel so lonely,
If only someone was there for me to turn to,
If there was only someone who understood,
Someone I could talk to, but I feel like everyone has left
Like, I am not good enough for them.
I am too broken and damaged for them to hang around,
They don't want to be seen with the girl who has scars,
The scars are hideous, and they make me ugly.
I feel so lonely,
I am too scared to tell, I just want to hide under the covers and never
    come out,
My life is torn, nothing is the same,
I just don't know what to do, don't know who I can talk to,
Seems like no one will listen, I am the girl who cries wolf in their eyes,
I am seeking attention.
They judge me, if they don't seem to mind, they don't seem to care,
They laugh, and they point.
I feel so lonely,
My heart is broken, it will never be the same, and my life has turned
    upside down,
I feel like I am falling,
What am I supposed to do, what can I do, who can I talk to?
No one seems to listen, I smile, I pretend
I am fine, what can I say, everyone is oblivious, they left,
I'm forgotten, and I mean nothing.
I overreact, I always do wrong, nothing is ever right,
I am drama, I lie, and I'm the problem,
I feel so lonely ...

Stephanie Hobart
Eau Claire, WI

Appreciation

I thank you Lord for hearing me
and showing that you care
Thank you Lord for going that last mile.
It was so very difficult
that I felt just like giving up—
then I looked up and saw your
lovely smile.

You're always there to see me through
and fill my every need,
you know the cravings of my soul.
Oh! Touch me Lord and make me whole
I'll praise your name and give my life to you.

My heart was broken, my spirit too
and no one seemed to care.
They just don't understand the way you do.
You're closer than a brother
and I know there is no other
that I can go and tell
my troubles to.

Aron Wooten
Hooks, TX

I wrote this poem in 1995 after a long battle with pancreatic cancer. When it was diagnosed, it was in its last stages and the doctor gave me six weeks to live. I prayed to ask God for healing, and I started getting better immediately. The doctor was amazed. I took no medication or treatments. I give God all the credit for everything.

When Life Is Found

I spoke to the rain gently tapping on my window,
"Bring forth ye gentle kiss and make my garden grow."

An old straw hat is perched like a bird on a fence post.
As the wind began to blow across the fields, I thought
I heard the voice of a pioneer calling out in the distance.

A faithful friend had come to visit and sit with me awhile.
What news is there from afar? I grow weary of television.

"The tree stands determined against the darkened horizon," he said.
It lays down its fruit so the deer may eat. But the deer are without
Knowledge of the future; they only pause to have their fill of food.
Yet we are not beasts, but human beings—made by the living God.

"Your words are gifts," I said. "For they impart true wisdom forgotten.
Come, let us pray to the God of heaven and earth that we may live."

Elliott Malm
McGrath, MN

Watch the Sky

Life is short and often filled with sorrow.
There is no promise of tomorrow.
Live each day with love and caring,
For those whose lives you're closely sharing.
It is by God's grace you live each day.
Trust in Him; all your fears He will allay.
Let Him hold you in His hand.
On your feet you'll squarely stand.
Bold and strong, defend the right,
And as you fall asleep at night,
Know that you have given
Your best measure of God's Heaven.
Smell the flowers, watch the sky—
For tomorrow you may die.

Gamaliel D. Phillips
Benson, AZ

Capt. Phillips flew jet fighters in the U.S. Airforce for eight years. He then was hired by United Airlines and flew for another twenty-seven years, retiring Jan. 1, 1992. As a young boy growing up in the hills of Eastern Kentucky, he had dreamed of a career in aviation. Dreams do come true! He wrote this poem in memory of his fellow pilots, their passengers, and all who lost their lives during this terrorist attack.

Ballad of Tom Carney

Not too many years ago,
There was phantom 309
And "Big Joe" was the name
But after "Big Joe" left us

To be with his heavenly Father,
In truck-driver Heaven
Then the Lord sent us another "hero"
He saved a dozen lives during his years

Behind the wheel of a big blue Mack truck
One day he was asking how he could be repaid
Right then he looks at his big blue Mack
Truck and Blue Mack came the answer

But, in the end he was just plain Tom Carney
A good man, and if you are going down that
Highway of life, and see old Tom, give
Him a big 10-4 for me. I will be seeing him

At the Lord's heavenly truck stop in the sky
with the Lord and the rest of the holy drivers
Alone with "Big Joe" and the phantom 309
"Oh yes," there will be Blue Mack there too
With the Lord in the sky

Charles E. Bullard
Lumberton, NC

*I am sixty-seven years old, and I live in Lumberton, NC. I wrote this poem
in 1984 while I was in prison. I read an article in the newspaper about truck
drivers always stopping and helping people. This driver was in a wreck and
died. I got the idea about the truck driver from the article I read. I put the
poem together, and the words started "clicking." I was a diesel mechanic for
sixteen years and then had a stroke. I enjoyed working on trucks. I was in the
army for fourteen years, during which I worked as a transportation specialist.
I am a Vietnam veteran.*

What Is a Poem?

A poem is morning's first light and twilight's last remains.
It is the happiness in change and the joy in "just the same."
It is destiny's knock and opportunity's open door.
It is the smell of spring and fall's desires to be more.

A poem is the reality of now and the best of past when.
It is the freshness of youth and the wish to begin again.
It is an older age and the wisdom to be shared.
It is a life alone and another to be paired.

A poem is you and me and everyone in between.
It is light and darkness ... the seen and the unseen.
It is time rushing rapidly and the clock's steady path.
It is words and sounds and truth that will last.

Jerome E. Howard
West Hartford, CT

My Master Cried Today

It was just like any Tuesday,
As I handed him my lead.
The morning sun was warm
With dancing colors for master and me.

As we ended our walk,
He took his seat.
He unfolded his paper,
As I curled up at his feet.

He "clicked" on the "talk box"
As usual every morn,
But today was different,
The voices were of alarm!

Can't understand the words
But the pictures were obvious,
Flying objects crashing into buildings,
People crying—no one would dare be callous!

For this Tuesday was dismal
As clouds of smoke appeared,
His heart was witness to the worst,
And the worst of all was fear.

His tears fell like rain.
Will the scenes ever fade?
For the first time I've ever known,
My master cried today!

Deborah A. Prine
Akron, OH

To My Loving Wife (True Love Never Dies)

True love never dies, it lasts
    through all eternity.
True love never dies, it will
    last for you and me.

My dear, you know I hate to go,
    you were my lover and my best friend.
Therefore I pray that someday
    I will see you again.

When you get lonely, think of only
    the good times that we knew.
Then a tear, will disappear, and
    a smile will come through.

For now, my dear, the time is here,
    for us to say our goodbyes.
Come hold my hand, you'll understand
    why true love never dies.

Darlin', our love was a true love,
    so please, please don't cry,
Because our love, was a true love
    that will never ever die.

True love never dies, it lasts
    through all eternity.
True love never dies, it will
    last for you and me.

Tom Eck
Tecumseh, KS

For My Mom

I hear your voice
In the train whistle
Announcing its presence.

I hear your voice
In the laughter
Of children playing.

I hear your voice
In the rustling of leaves
Falling to the ground.

I hear your voice
In the middle of the night
Softly whispering ... remember

Denise A. Vollbrecht
Waukesha, WI

Over the Rainbow, Above Every Star

To another land, someday I shall go
A place where milk and honey doth flow.
Our living Savior resides there now
When I enter that city, to Him I shall bow.

I'll look on the face of Jesus divine
Our master known to all, as the true living Vine
He's prepared a mansion for each for His own
I think mine is located right next to His throne.

I'll walk upon the streets of pure gold,
Then sit at His feet where mysteries unfold.
Jesus will tell us why He loves us so,
With the Holy Spirit among us, with our faces all aglow.

What a promise fulfilled on that blessed day,
We shall rejoice that we'd chosen God's way
Forever safe, in Heaven afar,
Over the rainbow, and above every star.

Lenia Whyel
Vacaville, CA

You Know Me

I give smiles in the sun.
I watch children play and run
I offer trails and paths to trod
Lofty trees, swimming pools and grassy sod
I may be the only place
Where some can find that peaceful space

I see people picnic on my lawn
Even little wildlife and gentle fawn
And you can come and leave worries behind
For I am forever in your mind
For ages and ages you have come to me
To play, to golf, to swim so merrily!

Return in spring and watch me grow
I'll never leave, I've told you so
Come in summer, my days are long
You'll sense my purpose, hear my song
Even in fall, when leaves are aflame
Hike a path ... play a good game

Yes of course, in winter amid the snow
I feel the blades of sleds that go
Yes, whenever you need me
To give your life a spark
Come and find me ...
I'm your neighborhood park!

June R. Truax
Cuyahoga Falls, OH

I am now an old lady—where did the years go? I have written poetry since my teens. Married to my husband Ralph for fifty-five years, we have three children, eight grandchildren, and seven great grandchildren. They are the focus of my life, but I do belong to the United Methodist Church, the Grange, Garden Club, Singing Seniors, Historical Society and work part-time as the security guard. I love my country and am a descendant of John Becklay, first Librarian of Congress. I reside in Cuyahoga Falls, OH.

Alzheimer's

Where have all our years gone, Love?
Through working, worrying, and laughing together
In fair and stormy weather
Through doubt and fears, death and tears,
With aging faces and slowing paces, we were one.
Is it possible you don't remember *us*?
Come back to me, Love.

Nina A. Olmsted
Jerseyville, IL

Love Comes Softly

Love is shy.
Love never asks why.
When you find true love
It is like a turtle dove.
Cooing and telling each other how you feel
I'm thinking can this be real
I've seen you walking by,
Strong and proud with head held high.
Love at first sight, has taken me to lofty heights.
I think of you night and day,
When we meet, what will I say?
From the heart for all to hear,
I love you my dear.

Norida Culp
Clifton, TX

By the Lake

He stands, staring into the lake
In the midst of the city,
A slight figure in plaid shirt and faded jeans;
Young, but hunched into himself
With the shrunken look of an old man
Caught in the sudden chill of late autumn.

The swish of cars passing on the street below
Come up to him—a sound in his ears
Like the brush of starched uniforms
Hurrying by in echoing halls.
On the horizon the sun sags into bloody strips
Of bandages. One isolated cloud, smooth and white,
Stands directly overhead, shining like
A sterile sheet in the mirror of the flat water.

He lingers, and as the lights from surrounding
Buildings come on one by one,
They swim in the reflected sky
Like golden luminarias along a half-forgotten way;
The stars themselves now sew
Tiny brilliants into the dark water.
He remembers other autumns, other nights
Under these same stars.

He stuffs his hands into his pockets,
For in the gathering night,
They are growing cold;
Much like the ones he lately clasped.

Pandora L. Wilson
Lakewood, CO

Untitled

On this cold winter's day
I sit and watch the leaves scurry by
heedless they are blown ...
tossed by the winds fickle temperament.

I think of thee—always—
when the wind blows and my heart aches.
My life's blood drips invisibly upon the pavement.
In sorrow and in hope
I long to hear from thee
even one word—a sigh perhaps—
directed towards me.

Your intermittent presence
I greedily gulp down like a dying man
who, parched by drought, ravishedly drinks salt water
thinking it sweet in comparison.
Drink thy foolish soul drink.
Drink while you still can!

You are salt water to me—and I blindly drink of thee.
In utter contentment my thirst is abated—for the moment ...

Only when you are absent from me
do you realize
I am left thirstier—than I ever was before—and it is
sweet torment.

I am not—nor will I ever be ...
satisfied.

Mary L. Haydon
Vepoe Bay, OR

Tiffany

They decided long ago, their jobs were more important so
Children were the last thing on their minds,
All wrapped up in their careers, kids would only interfere,
All they saw were big green dollar signs.

Now twenty years have passed them by, and still no family,
What they wouldn't give to hold a baby on their knee.

She'd love buying baby clothes, they're tired of feeling so alone,
A high chair and a baby stroller too,
A crib, some toys, and baby food, to fill that empty lonesome room,
Freshly painted walls of pink or blue.

It didn't take the agency, but just a month or two,
To find the sweetest baby girl that heaven ever grew.

Little babies sleep so much, they can't wait 'til she wakes up,
They just want to hold her all the time,
No greater love could ever be, than the love they have for Tiffany.
Life is now the perfect nurs'ry rhyme.

Glenn Smith
Jacksonville, FL

The Snow

The snow falls gently down on the ground in front of me
As the day goes on, I watch the snow and start to think of him

I think of the way he used to look at me
I think of the sound of his voice
I think of when he used to talk to me all the time

As I know it will never be the same the memories
         start to fade away
Knowing he will never love me

The snow still falls harder and harder

Suddenly a figure appears in the snow
As he approaches he looks familiar
Then I realize who he is
Now he disappears

Now my mind wanders off and I forget completely
         about him
Never truly did he exist
Just my imagination
Never will I forget the man I used to think of
Never will I forget how he broke my heart
I will always love him

Sydney Schryer
Upper Sandusky, OH

An Angel

If I could make an angel,
To walk upon the Earth,
I'd make an angel,
With an ordinary birth.

To experience the trials of life,
Pain, almost everyday,
But to always rise above,
In her own amazing way.

To grow up and fall in love,
To experience real hurt.
Then have her marry the love of her life,
But who can be a real jerk.

And yet she loves me everyday,
I that amazing angel way.

If I could make an angel
To walk upon the Earth,
I would name her Joan,
O the day of her birth.

Eric Dymesich
Mason, WI

Unforeseen

It's all unexpected, isn't it,
the morning that creeps across the bridge
then raptures in sun-splashes and raven wings,
or the rain that slicks along the pavement,
then sputters around lovers' feet?

People, too, turn you inside out,
quicker than an eye-blink,
or a flash of swan's down:
the brilliant *abuelo* who cannot read;
the imperious dancer looking out of eyes
abused, bruised in darkened rooms.

All of it, blaze and black, sky and soil,
enfolds opposites that straggle and stream
crossing our day's borders.
Yet I wouldn't want the everyday walled
against impetuous possibilities of storm-raging seas,
loves discovered in moments caught unbidden,
dances flashing unforeseen.

Kathy Parker Blount
Watsonville, CA

The Darker, the Danker, the Better

The darker, the danker, the better. Pour me, poor me, a drink.
I came here to drown my fear and not to bloody think.
And who the hell are you to say that you feel my pain?
I'm the one who did the damage, and yes, I am insane.

A cold day in December as I stumbled from that bus,
I'd lost my sense of balance, fell, and I began to cuss.
"I know this town, I know it well," at least I told myself.
"But will I be all right this time?" buzzed feelings on a shelf.

There may be a relapse, another one in me.
Yes, there may be a relapse with no recovery.
So to these rooms I do come and I sit and stay.
And to these rooms I will come to fight another day.

"We do not shoot our wounded," said the woman oh so kind.
"Come sit here, attempt good cheer, your wounds then shall we bind."
"As you rest and talk with us you will plainly see
That as you sit and share with us your God shall set you free."

Another room, another place, still in this same old town,
Bad rental space all in my head, too much of that abounds.
A cold night in December, and as we gathered there
Humbly we bowed our heads and closed our group in prayer.

Robert Kellogg
Denver, CO

The Perfect Pair

Lo and behold!
Just over the ridge,
there was the perfect find
that could really be mine.

In the misty morning sunshine,
there stood an armchair
sparkling in blue
and looking brand new.

A remnant of someone else's past,
the chair was no longer wanted.
Simply chucked to the side
because its owner had died.

So the chair sat
all bewildered with dew.
Marked free for the taking
and the cost of the lugging.

That was fine with me.
I stopped for a closer look,
and am pleased to share,
the chair had been handled with care.

I snatched it up quickly
and brought it home.
A match was made
between the chair and me,
and proven once again:
the best things in life are free.

Diana Buehl
Hankins, NY

Jennifer

What a beautiful baby girl you are.
You are the best at everything you do by far.
You're so precious, as precious as the brightest shining star.
I love you Jennifer just as you are.

You're so kind and caring,
always sharing
there is just no comparing.

Don't ever forget me, you mean so much
Don't know what I'd do without you I need you a bunch!

I want to always be there for you in good times and in bad.
Come talk with me anytime happy or sad.
I love you Jennifer, I want to be the best friend you ever had.

Tara Whisman
Big Timber, MT

I wrote this poem for all the love I have for my beautiful daughter, for all that she was and all that she is. Writing this poem for my daughter Jennifer is a very special way to show my love for her, in life and eternal life. I love you, Jennifer, and I am the luckiest mom in the world.

Beneath the Evergreen

Although He called you home so soon,
Your gentle spirit seen,
Whene'er I walk in solitude,
Beneath the evergreen.

Take comfort here to know that you
Now tend His grove of pine
Where breezes warmly soothe the soul,
And sun forever shines.

When passing verdant rows of yew
I'll gaze the azure sky,
And feel your quiet presence here,
To lift my spirit high.

When near the spruce and juniper
I'll amble there a while,
And think of cherished mem'ries shared,
And see your caring smile.

When 'neath the hemlock canopy
He'll call to comfort me,
And whisper softly you're at peace,
For sweet eternity.

So meet me when He calls me home—
Eternal rest serene.
Our spirits walk together then,
Beneath the evergreen.

Dennis E. Black
Thurmont, MD

The poet wrote this poem in memory of his cousin Richard Daniel Pryor who was born on August 11, 1971 and lost at sea on August 27, 2005.

Untitled

Love will come again; I shan't lose hope.
Someday I know I'll find
The one my heart is longing for;
Our souls fore'er to bind.

Whether in a face I know so well,
Or one I've yet to see.
I'll find the hand that fits in mine,
As if 'twas meant to be.

Then all will seem to sweetly fit;
The puzzle now intact.
We'll have no memory of days before;
No trace of what we lacked.

And I will joy in his embrace
Until I've breathed my last.
For I trust that we will meet again,
When all the days have passed;
In Heaven's gates at last ...

Rebecca Stump
Hellertown, PA

Snowflakes

Swirling, floating, dancing,
No two the same.
Harshness of winter romancing,
Identity only in name.

Interlocking finally as they settle
Forming a single temporary bond,
Covering harvest field and hedgerow nettle
Blanket on woodlot, uniform on frozen pond.

Uncompromising gray day,
Extending bleak and gloom,
Shrouding in solemn reverent way,
Every picket fence and tomb.

Brilliant sparkling crystals,
Representing long forgotten souls,
Eulogizing forgotten epistles,
Muffled ring as the bell tolls.

Life, dormant in frozen womb,
Inanimate in stately repose,
Ransoming warm rains of June,
Now animating new life's ethos.

Transforming the new season,
Melted droplets overrun the banks to the hinterland,
Faded memory aiding the existing reason,
We anticipate the cycle producing the winterland.

Ruben Beedle
Cle Elum, WA

The World in Reality

Everything changes,
Everything remains the same.
The clouds shift, the weather moves, the thunder cracks a time or two,
But everything remains the same.
The buildings rise, oceans change tides, people tell lies,
But everything remains the same.
Some are hurt, some are strong. Some just keep trudging along,
But everything remains the same.
She looks forward, he looks back. They go onto different paths,
But everything remains the same.
People cry, people survive, and everything remains the same.
Why?
Only one person can handle themselves, if more is tried,
Everything will change.
Or everything will remain the same,
And no one knows which one is worse.

Anna Hightower
Cartersville, GA

It's Time to Grow

Let go of your worries
Leave the past behind.

It's time to move forward,
and capture your dreams.

Living in the present,
starting to grow.

With each moment,
hoping to loosen the load.

Reach out for tomorrow
by finding today.

Moving forward as
the day passes away,

Then in the evening,
reflect on the day,

in hope that tomorrow
will bring more
growth your way.

Adam Dehner
Franklin, PA

Live Your Life

No matter what age you've got to live your life
That means listening to yourself more than others
And doing what makes you happy
Living life like it's your last day
Even if you don't have enough pay
Making each moment a memory you'll never forget
Like it's that special person you've just met
Put to use the talents that you were given
So you have nothing to be forgiven
Even trying your best can lead to disappointment
It doesn't mean you're a failure
Roadblocks only make you stronger
Rolling with the punches makes you live longer
Confidence is key to living your life
It let's you get over your fears
Sometimes the best things in life are free
These are your family and friends
It doesn't cost anything to keep them
And they help you feel better about yourself
Material things can't replace love
They can only make you happy in the short-term
You must follow your heart and do the best things for you
Not everyone is good at everything
Each person is made differently
The key is to do what you like
If you like what you do then you'll be successful

Daniel Tommasi
Kennebunk, ME

Pastoral Poem

I think I might live a dream for an hour,
 Escaping the madness of phone calls and paperwork,
 Soaking up the beaming sun and wrapping myself in the warm sand.

I will gaze out to shore on a crisp autumn day,
 Tasting the salty air as it stings my lips,
 Watching the waves crash and hearing their roar,
 Pushing my thoughts to the back of my mind.

With no crowds to avoid I keep myself company,
 Listening to the voices of the seagulls,
 Walking on the damp sand,
 Brushing against the water as it edges towards my toes.

Maybe for an hour I will treat myself to pure bliss,
 Forgetting about the "hellos" and "please holds"
 Living in a simple paradise,
 Where the days are long and the nights are short.

I will regain reality letting go of my paradise,
 And sigh in harmony with the wind.

Olivia I. Sacco
Madison, CT

To the Bride and Groom

Oh, the happy wedding day
Takes all your doubts and fears away!
Problems and cares together your face,
Will soon disappear at a rapid pace.
It proves that love really does pay
In an overwhelming and glorious way.
And in today's whirlwind of life, one's fate
Needs an honest, dependable, steady-going mate.
These qualities you both seem to already share
Which proves to all that you really care.
However,there will be times when you disagree.
That is when you will really see
If love is patient, love is kind,
And can even be a little blind!
Ah yes, this exciting venture,marriage,will prevail
Much longer than a hot-air balloon flight
Or climbing the Appalachian Trail.
And so, family members and good friends here today
Wish you health and happiness as you travel life's way.
And I predict that amid laughter and tears
This journey, together, will last through the years!

Helen Simpson
Mount Airy, MD

I have always loved poems that rhyme. I believe this developed when, as a young mother, I read nursery rhymes to my children each night at bedtime. Later I wrote short poems of my family and friends, young and old, and in all walks of life. Some verses to provoke laughter, others to praise accomplishments. Every year my Christmas card is a decorated page with a poem relating my year's activities. It is my way of staying connected to all. I am now ninety-six years old and was so pleased when my granddaughter requested a few words at her wedding!

Personality

When we are born in this world we are giving a personality that is our
    own.
So that we can show God in every way that He is, and when we take
    on someone else's personality we change God in us.
And we lose ourself and the gift that God gave only to us.
So be yourself and show God in you.
So the gift that God gave us will show in your personality.

JoAnn Fulbright
Ft. Smith, AR

Burn Fire Burn

The gnarled body
Limbs stiff and projecting up and out
Nude and bare
No cover for decency
Once a long living beautiful creation
Now lifeless in the middle of a field
Its consciousness having drifted into the unknown
A complicated stump
That man considers nothing
A lovely tree soon leaving this world

Annabelle Abegglen Apodaca
Medford, OR

A Sense-sational World

Smelling a rose that's been newly cut,
    Enjoying the taste of a freshly roasted nut,
Sounds of a fire truck passing by
    Tasting freshly baked apple pie, oh my!
Sun's heat on your back as you lay on the sand
    The gritty feel of sand clinging to your hand
Gently lapping water as a boat passes by
    Blue sky with puffy white clouds up so high!
Symphony music enjoyed by any ear
    Noisy fireworks as a holiday draws near.
Feeling materials in a dressmaker's shop
    A policeman's whistle bringing traffic to a stop.
Wondrous odors when visiting a perfume show
    Majestic mountains covered in glistening snow
High-flying jets screaming overhead
    The warmth of a wool blanket on my comfy bed.
Watching a candle's wax drip down its side
    Putting hands over my eyes to play hide
Taking the dog for a good long walk
    Having time to greet a neighbor and talk.

Virginia Fuhr
Oviedo, FL

I'm a senior citizen who enjoys putting pen to paper. Being retired I do have the opportunity to create my own canvas, as often as I want and when I want. Words fascinate me and I enjoy arranging and changing them to my own satisfaction. Not only does it give me something fulfilling to do in my golden years, but hopefully it gives me a creative avenue that I can explore whenever and however I want. New avenues are just waiting to be explored. Why don't you try some!

Pet Rabbit

There once was a shy little rabbit,
Try as they may, no one could grab it.
He hopped here and there,
He hopped most everywhere.
He liked eating flowers,
He ate flowers for hours.
The shy rabbit had no name,
And he surely wasn't tame.
He didn't have a home,
It seemed all he did was roam.
One day as he hopped for joy,
He spotted a scared little boy.
As the rabbit hopped to get near,
It became perfectly clear,
That the boy was sad and alone.
He longed for a pet of his own.
The boy gave a sad little sigh,
When the rabbit came nearby,
He liked the rabbit with no name,
And the rabbit felt the same.
Just as the boy started to leave,
The rabbit tugged on his sleeve.
He followed the little boy home,
Because he no longer wanted to roam.

Delores Jabaay
Connell, WA

I've always enjoyed poetry and sometimes words just come into my head. I especially enjoy writing children's poems. I guess the reason for that may be because we have four grown children and fourteen grandchildren.

Her Elegance So Sweet

To hath met and perceived—
A beauty so glorious, I hath dreamed!

Her eyes, a sea of life,
Mightily flowing through my chest:
I hath no word, no notion, that could illustrate
This passion I doth address!

How genuine, her soul—
And oh! how vast her faith!
She is a woman who cherishes
The gift of grace.

From her lips comes truth
(My heart flutters at the sound!)—
And I cannot cease my gaze,
As to her mine eyes are bound.

Oh, how magnificent—truly, how serene!—
Is her loveliness, as though from a dream I hath dreamed!

Tyler Eskovitz
South Lyon, MI

Some Dreams Must Die

While out having breakfast one glorious Friday morning -
I sensed some movement out the corner of my right eye.
I looked up and saw you near my table passing by.
I didn't know I've missed you with such longing, yearning.
Till I heard from somewhere near this haunting and soulful cry.
Then realized it was my own voice calling softly your name.

You have chosen a table directly behind me.
I was ready to go; should I turn around and say hello?
My deep and heavy sigh expressed my "no" reply.
Halfway to the door, I slowly looked behind me.
Our eyes met and locked, which seemed like eternity.
In that precious moment, my heart melted and my eyes said "good-bye."

Longing and yearning for you have just been dreams.
Perhaps someday, as years go by, some dreams may die.

Erlinda Rizada Hagemeyer
Rochelle, IL

Love Heart

As the sun rises
and sets so does
my heart
My dearest love when
I breathe to exist
this heart bleeds
within
Time passes by as
my heart grows
In pain while
the wind blows
my heart
The stars shine
as my heart
goes on

PJ Olivas
Needville, TX

WMA

You are our mothers and blessed we are;
Without you we could not have come so far.

You give us help, trust and love;
Just like our heavenly Father, from above.

The counselors' jobs are made easier,
Knowing you care;
All the trouble, trials and joy you share.

You have helped make GMA
A great place to be;
Counselors and girls alike give
Our thanks to thee.

Our WMA mothers,
This tribute we give to you;
Included is our love
And appreciation too.

Beth Wallace
Greenbrier, AR

Untitled

Sunflowers are smiling
to the sunlight
Grass is waving
lazily
Birds are singing
bright and cheerful
Filling the meadow
with melody

Hannah Ruth Hershberger
Millersburg, OH

God's Heartbeat

If you could hear God's heartbeat
What would you hear:
The rustling of leaves on an autumn's morn,
The rise and fall of a baby's breath,
The tinkling of a wind chime against the lull of the sea,
The soft flutter of linens on a summer's line,
The laughter of a child,
The crackle of a fire deep into the night,
The soft voices of your parents as you're nodding off to sleep?
Lean in close,
Rest your weary ear,
Can you hear it?

Michele Gunsauls
Red Bluff, CA

A Morning Prayer

Dear Lord,

Help me be a faithful servant today
In all that I do and all that I say.

May each thought be pleasing, dear Father above;
Fill me Holy Spirit, as I walk in your love.

Then when trouble comes and I'm tossed on life's tide,
My heart will remember you walk by my side ...

And when that day comes and I see face to face
My precious Lord Jesus who poured out His grace,

I will hear those sweet words, "Faithful servant, well done.
You've fought the good fight, the hard race you have run.

Now enter my rest, come sit at my knee,
We'll enjoy each other's presence throughout eternity."

Yes, let it be so, Lord, as I praise you again.
Your name be glorified, Lord.

Amen and Amen

Sylvia J. DeVita
Mountain Rest, SC

Modern-Day Judas

A strange man
walks into a strange town
down a strange street
into a strange house

He enters a strange room
walks up to a strange window
pulls out a familiar gun
aiming it out that strange window

Across the way stands a familiar figure
on a strange hotel balcony

The strange man pulls the familiar trigger
aiming at that familiar figure

B A N G

Martin Luther King is dead

Mary Miller
Belvidere, IL

Barefoot and Sunglasses

Playing in a neighbor's yard
Whiffle ball
Lying in the grass
Barefoot
Swimming in a creek
Cut-offs
Clearing a path
Grapevines
Enjoying a drink
Garden hose
Playing at a local park
Baseball
Lying on a lawn chair
Sunglasses
Swimming in a pool
Swim trunks
Clearing a trail
Four-wheeler
Enjoying a drink
Bottled water
Me as a child
My son now
Has so much really changed?
Or has so much stayed the same?

Pamela Irene McDonald
Saxton, PA

I live in Coalmont, PA with my husband, David, and son, Mitchell. I was inspired to write the poem as I thought about Mitchell turning seventeen and being a senior in high school. Life seems to have so many challenges for the youth of today, and, despite what many people think, I believe kids are not so different than they were years ago. I also love sharing poetry with my third-grade students and want them to see that I love writing in my spare time.

She

She's a river of love,
And a mountain of hope.
She knows what to say,
When I just cannot cope.
She brings a kind of promise,
To my old weary heart.
The way she does soothe me,
It must be an art.
She's there when I'm happy,
And there when I'm sad.
She's there just to be there,
And man am I glad.
She lifts up my being,
And makes me feel new.
If she got to know you,
You would feel the same too.
She brings out my human,
To the best it can be
For my life to flourish
There can only be she.

Bobby J. Skipper
Lowell, NC

Machismo

Ancient ritual of father and son
Reluctant gladiators,
Facing each other across the years
With blood leaking from the wounds of our yesterdays,
And tears that drench the soul and not the cheek.
Beginning our flight with thumbs down,
We look at each other through windows of lead.

While each waits for the other to speak
Words die in the heart and rot the brain—
Malignancies of our inheritance
That state a man must be a man
Never knowing it takes a man to cry.
God, reach down and touch the hand of Adam
Before we bruise the night with parings of our soul.

Wayne Newberry
Ft. Worth, TX

God's Care

With the angels looking on,
Standing at your feet,
You are now forever in your sleep.

The friends and family you
Have left behind,
Are never far away, now God is at your side.

We won't forget the day you left,
Out of our lives you have crept.

In the distance you hear faint cries,
We'll always remember how you
Touched our lives.

As the days go on you are remembered
With a sigh
Of all the happiness of days gone by.

To us at times life isn't fair,
Only God knows he's in our prayers.

The love and laughter you have shown,
For now you roam around God's home.

As a river flows safely to the sea,
Forever in God's care you will always be.

Donna Fauske
Columbia Falls, MT

In the Potter's Hands

Mold me to fit Your divine plan,
Lord, You're the potter, I'm the clay.
Keep me pliable as You work
Until I yield in every way.

Throw me upon Your potter's wheel.
Cut away parts that are untrue.
Centering my life in Your word,
Form my vessel to honor You.

Let the water of Your spirit
Wash and soften my stubborn heart,
Shaping my life with caring hands,
'Til I'm who You'd planned from the start.

Don't leave me on the potter's wheel,
But in life's kiln test my resolve.
Give me the strength that will withstand
All that living for You involves.

An untried vessel's of no use,
Untested servants doubly so.
Submit me to the trials of life
That I may learn, and in You grow.

Fill me with godly character
So that wherever I may be,
As by word and deed I serve You,
The master potter's all they'll see.

Carol S. Huffman
Rochester, IN

The Life of Tyler

I go to sleep when it's night.
I wake up to the morning light.
I like to drink Sprite.
I like to fly a kite.
I never like to fight.
I have a good sight.
Sometimes I have the might.

Tyler Milton George Ammons
Newberry, SC

I am nine years old. I have an older sister who is ten and a younger brother who is four. My father is deceased and we live with my mother in Newberry, SC. I like to draw and I love riding my dirt bike at the "Brick House" in Laurens, SC.

A Legacy: A Quiet Life

She sits so helpless, gaunt and still;
independent care exists!
She seems so common where she lies,
as workers often missed her gaze.
So many pass throughout her day;
but did they notice? Did they say—
What of this woman's history,
before her current misery?
She is and was and will always be
the constant star that guided me.
But often as a child I mused—
No time for games to win or lose.
Could she not play, could she not laugh?
The meals were made, the clothes were clean;
but time was gone—no "in-between!"
But now I understand the gaff.
Her work was never, ever done—
She toiled and worked til setting sun.
No thanks was given and none expected—
She gave from grit her mom perfected!
And so the legacy she gives—
A life for me to better live!
A lot less strain, a lot less stress,
and thanks to Mom who gave her best!
She stirs my heart as I leave her door—
She is my mom, but *so much more!*

Nancy Wagner
Clayton, WI

Having managed a congregate care facility, and also having grown up with my grandmas, I know well the quietness of the elderly experience; no one asks who they were and are as they endure such humiliation when their minds and bodies betray them! Now faced with my own mother's fate anguishing in a nursing home, away from everything that defines her, in quietness, she endures the indignities of this plight. I want my poem to speak for all those cloistered away, plead for their dignity and remember their essence—what they have contributed to our legacy—a quiet life, ringing loudly of strength!

One Day

To my daughter, while you're finding your way,
I have a few special words I'd like to say.
No matter what you've said or done,
You will now and always have my love.
You may have regrets over your past,
But God's forgiveness will forever last.
I pray one day that you will see,
Just how beautiful life can be.
I know you've felt a lot of sadness and pain,
And often I take on some of the blame.
You have chosen a path that's been downhill,
The drugs, defiance, rebellion, cheap thrills.
I pray one day that you will see,
Just how beautiful life can be.
I see you in your young son's eyes,
And your noninvolvement makes me cry.
At family dinners there's your empty seat,
But I'm not, and I won't give in to defeat.
I pray one day that you will see,
Just how beautiful life can be.
I have my faith and prayers, each day anew,
And hopefully you will one day too.
So as the mornings come and the evenings pass,
I pray your destructive choices won't last.
I pray one day that you will see,
Just how beautiful life can be.

Cynthia Morris
Eureka, CA

My name is Cynthia Morris. I reside in Northern California among the majestic Redwood trees. I've written poems periodically throughout my life. I read about this contest but couldn't create anything new, so I sadly accepted I wouldn't be entering. One night at church this poem came pouring our of me. I've been thanking God daily. Recent trials in my life inspired this poem. I'm a blessed daughter, wife, mother, and grandmother. I am grateful for this contest, to have this poem published instead of being hidden in a dark drawer for no one to see.

I Am

I am simply not you
I wonder why I have to explain myself
I hear, but my mind is usually on a different shelf
I see the world from my own view
I am simply not you

I pretend that I've survived all this wear
I feel so much but I am still left bare
I touch the hearts of as many as I can
I worry that no one else understands
I cry when I sympathize with the things people do
I am simply not you

I understand that we live in a world that's fallen away
I say, "I love you," to my girl every day
I dream of what the world could be
I try to pray for everybody
I hope that ... *no* ... I just don't want to
I am simply not you

Corey Rouse
Nekoosa, WI

Sometimes

Into our lives come many moments to treasure,
many moments to ponder and also to measure.
Sometimes we wonder if we should open the door
to allow ourselves to go down this new road of more.
Sometimes we hesitate to allow the heart to be touched
and then we step back and say we can't be rushed.
Sometimes we think things over too much
while we wrestle with past hurts and such.
But then, sometimes we take the hand of our Lord
and begin to trust in His wisdom to bring one accord.
Those are the sometimes we grow by and in moments like these
we are blessed to be made free ... free to see that He is pleased.

Charlene Dargatz
Mayville, WI

*The information for this poem came from a real-life circumstance in the life
of Charlene. She loves to write about real-life situations, and the real author
of the poems is her Lord and Savior. He is her inspiration and her guide and,
in the long run, is especially discerning as she learns from him about real-life
emotions and what to do with them. To that end, she is dedicated and will
always continue to grow in Him.*

An Old Cowboy's Dream

Oh! How I wish I could play cowboy again.
Just to be around a horse, the way it was way back then.
The scent from the horse, the fur and swishing
tail. Just the anticipation of riding the trail.
Brushing, curing, the saddling up. Bridle
next, reins around her mane, while fitting the
boot in the old stirrups.
One swing and I'm in the cup—but age
age twelve, that's a long way up.
"Patches" was her name, with a brown and
white silky mane. I lift off the saddle and
lean forward a bit. Swift and smooth
she takes the bit. Off we go her mane
and tail a-flying. With wind in my face
making tears like I'm crying. Over the hill and
down and over tree stumps: Wow! I can
feel my heart jump. She's run enough, time
to slow, take it easy—her head still snapping
ready to go. She sure worked up a sweat that's
drippin' wet. Hold back those reins and get her to slow
prancing and dancing these things she knows. We sure had
a lot of fun, making that run. Now I'm just talking
as I go back to bed. But she understood every word I said.

Richard Waters
Yucca Valley, CA

Father's Day

Happy Father's Day to my very best friend.
The one whom with the rest of my life,
I want to spend.
I've always said you are wonderful,
This I know to be true.
I am truly blessed to have fallen in love
with you.
You make my days happier, my heart
skips a beat.
With you in my life, my dreams are
always sweet.
I'm not the only one that knows how
special you are.
In your children's eyes, you are
their shinning star.
I've never met a daddy that has
measured up to you.
On this special day and always, I see
their love shine through.
Always remember, you mean the world
to them and to me.
There is no place in the world, than with you,
that I would rather be.

Sheila Durden
Demopolis, AL

My name is Sheila Oliver Durden. I am forty-two years old from Demopolis, AL. I have two wonderful daughters, Makayla and Mckenzie. "Father's Day" was written for my very best friend, Tony, whom I love with all of my heart, so every holiday, special occasion, his birthdays or just because, I put pen to paper and the words flow. "Father's Day" is one of the many poems inspired by him. I am blessed to have this special talent and consider myself fortunate to have Tony as my very best friend and inspiration.

The Bronco

I was at the rodeo
I had on my hat
It was my turn on the bronco
I rode it 8 seconds flat

The bronc was so mad
That I was still on its back
That it winnowed and bucked
Throwing me off on my hat

Ryan Stinson
Prescott, AZ

I live in Prescott, AZ, home of the world's oldest rodeo. I went to my first rodeo this year, and wrote this poem. I was invited to read my poem at the Arizona Cowboy Poets Gathering. I was honored to be one of five kids chosen to perform.

My Mother

Oh mother of mine, I thank God everyday for the gift that he sent me, a beautiful bouquet. Flowers that bloom everyday of the year enclosed in a golden vase that will forever endure. A bouquet of flowers sent by God from the heavens and delivered by angels, his loving servants.

For Mother, it should be very plain to see, you are the bouquet of flowers God sent to me. May peace and joy fill up your every day, may happiness and love always be your way. You are that very special gift from God, a bouquet of flowers, a gift of love.

Clifford Carl LaRue
Davenport, WA

I grew up on a farm in Eastern Washington State. In 1981 I moved to the great state of Alaska and graduated from the University of Alaska in 1990. I have always loved writing and poetry just became natural to me. Mostly I like to write poems about love. I also enjoy writing children's books. Currently I have two self-published editions about the "Three Little Alaskan Princesses." Two other editions are currently waiting to be illustrated. I love life and many more new and exciting poems and books will follow into my journey. God bless!

Scenes of the Seasons

A morning walk to smell,
Fragrance of new daffodils,
and feel dew drops that fell,
Showers came on the hills.

Long days mean more fun,
Watching butterflies and bees,
Feeling hot rays from sun,
Hearing birds sing in trees.

Cooler daybreaks come soon,
Leaves' colors are red and brown,
Yellow goldenrods bloom,
Orange pumpkins cover ground.

Icebergs hang from gutters,
Soft snow flakes fill the sky,
Birds hunt food as they flutter,
Whirling cold wind comes by.

Edith M. Biddix
Marion, NC

I started writing simple poetry in school. It was a gift from God. I like to read poetry by other authors. I have been a member of a North Carolina Poetry Society and Christian Writer's League. I have had poems published in our local newspaper. I am listed in the Who's Who Book for Authors and Writers. The National Library of Poetry published one poem in the book: On the Threshold of a Dream. My inspiration for the poem "Scenes of the Seasons" was my love for nature and its beauty.

My Best Friend

Comfort and peace were her gifts to me;
her little sweet self.
She hung on my every word and I loved her thoughtful silence;
adoring companions.
Thankfulness and praise in a lovely forest paradise;
our earthly Heaven.
Content with our simple existence, I didn't realize
my grave situation; my slow demise.
So heartbroken by her sudden death; deep despair.
A shattered life has no need for a lung transplant;
no will to live.
Daily prayer and time helped to soothe the pain;
brighter days ahead.
Her death was not my undoing but an awakening;
my epiphany.
Beautiful new lungs will herald a life of healthy freedom;
my second wind.
A daily struggle to breathe, I pray it's not much longer;
so sick and weary.
Remembering my heavenly girl brings a smile;
her little sweet self.

Johanna Libbert
Richland, IN

*As you may have guessed, my best friend was a dog. Dogs are the most
wonderful beings God created. Because of Ebony, the next dog I adopt
will be named Joy. I am married to an equally wonderful man (twenty-four
years). I have cystic fibrosis and am awaiting a double-lung transplant.*

Sugar

I remember a time when I was a kid
I wanted to be a cowgirl, I did!
I desired to learn to rope and to ride.
I wanted a horse not an old donkey hide.
But the donkey I got and mean she sure was
And me all dressed up in my pretty "cow duds."
I'd hop on her back and head down the road
Not knowing she desired to unburden her load.
Sooner than later I'd find myself flying.
Flat on my back in the dusty road lying.
With an equine smirk and a snort from her snout
At me she was laughing there wasn't a doubt.
Everyone wondering if I was ok
On her I would mount the very next day.
The bucking, the "broncing," the squalling, the falling
Most of the time I found myself bawling!
As time progressed on I rode many a horse.
I didn't forget the donkey of course.
But two things I never got straight in my head,
That I was alive and never found dead.
And secondly about that mean, hairy booger
Why in the world did we call her Sugar?

Susan Alvis
Bryan, TX

I Won

No spinning the wheel
No game boards
No scratch-five
No computer
No cyber space
No electronics
No solar
No magic!

I won, I have the source
I won, I listened, and I obeyed
I won, I have the gift
I won, I have wisdom
I won, I trusted, I made a choice.

I won, I am determined
I won, I am steadfast
I won, I have a purpose
I won, I have great expectations
I won, I am courageous.

I won because I had a promise
I had competition
I had bystanders
I had fault finders ...

Yet, I still won; because—
The greater power lives in me!

Florence P. Holloway
Spring Grove, VA

My Dream

I have this strong idea
Of a cookbook I'd like to make.
There'd be a need for workers
To help us learn to bake.

We need those books to remember
Those goodies from a long time back,
When moms and grammies did their thing,
And they really had the knack.

They may have had a measuring cup,
But didn't use it much.
A "pinch" of this and "some" of that,
Made it perfect to the touch.

The book is not for only Mom,
But Dad can use it too.
The kids also can join right in
And show what they can do.

Some good "old friends," who have passed on
Will always be around,
When we "whip up" their recipes,
Their memories abound.

Each recipe is a favorite
Of someone who loves it too,
And we hope a few of these
Will become a favorite for you.

Emma M. Repp
Emmaus, PA

Riding the Wind

When I ride the wind,
I sweep through the trees,
Sound like the ocean,
And whisper through leaves.

I rustle through hair
And stir up the dust.
I lift up girls' skirts
By forming a gust.

I carry the scent
Of man to a deer,
Helping it escape
Somewhere in the rear.

I rush up ridges
And ruffle the lakes
And bring on the storms
That thunder and quake.

I flow through the shade
Where shadows are deep
And cool the workers
Who seek rest or sleep.

I wave the flags of
Every known nation,
Yet I never know
My destination.

Ronald D. Lee
Spokane, WA

The Tree Outside My Window

To anyone passing by, this tree seems like just another old tree.
It stands outside my window and is very special to me.
Pepaw pointed it out to me as we walked in the pasture one day,
he told me it could help me understand things as I went along life's way.
He told me to be grounded with strong and mighty roots,
with the things that matter—God, family, kindness, honesty, integrity,
and not what the world suits.
This tree, he said, is always reaching higher to achieve its very best,
to reach its goal it must keep on, later there will be time for rest.
It reaches out to those around it and shelters the very small,
it gives a place to lean, a place of shade—it cares for us all.
He told me to be the one who reaches out to others,
we are put here to help those around us, we should all be brothers.
This tree rejoices with each sunrise and we should do the same.
Encourage someone, be a safe place to land, make sure others know
your name.
This space outside my window is occupied by a tree,
it makes a difference in the world around it, just by being a tree.
I want to make a difference, just by being me.
My pepaw is gone now, it is time for him to rest,
but he made a difference while he was here, he chose to give his best.
How you live your life is a choice, this we all know.
Sometimes great things can be learned from the tree outside your
window.

Garrett Larson
Mannsville, OK

What inspired my poem was my pepaw. He loved the land and the creatures in it. He was a farmer. He believed in living life for God and with integrity. He taught his kids and grandkids to live life that way too. I hope when I'm old I can look back and see that I have lived the words of my poem. I live in the country and enjoy archery and karate in my spare time. I plan to be a vet someday and take care of animals.

Refracted Memories

Painting still-life,
with a real brush
really fashions intent
with starlight bent

never broken, and yet
never received properly;
so goes the ways
of the times of smiles,

with pure aged perfection
and wispy winter reflection;
how the time passes, and how
many laughs did we share?

we were all together,
so many years ago
seems like yesterday;
the time, the light is pure

for reflected light is the
past again received;
I look back on the many
memories and smile again ... relieved!

Thomas L. Jackson
Ft. Gibson, OK

What Grows in Brooklyn?

Joyce Kilmer wrote the poem "Trees"
Such quality one seldom sees

That reaches up beyond the skies
To the heavens and never dies

Those leafy branches seen to pray
So promised me a better day

Until I recalled with a shock—
There were no trees upon my block

Joseph Flynn
Aiken, SC

What is a ramble? I will tell. What starts the thing, what rings the bell. It begins with a distant urge and grows to an insistent surge. Opinion, truth, or the absurd—beginning line, or just a word. Sometimes a thought brings me onto a road I walk that leads me to a conclusion I did not know before I knew where it would go. Then, as some roads are want to do, a turn-around adjusts my view, where I trended I won't end up—word flow was stopped by a hiccup. And when, at last, I think I'm done, O. Henry finish caps the fun, then serious and weighty tomes are out the window in my poems.

Hoochiemama Queen

Hoochiemama Queen, come by me, what do you mean?
Stand up straight and erect, tell me your dream!
Why such an attitude and callous look?
You are mistaking me for your negative hook.
That is not me nor my motto or aim!
For I've come to show you what heights you can
gain. The level of accomplishment you're able to
claim. Erase your ghetto slang of yeh, uh hah,
I ain't got no name and replace it with, I love
what God has placed on this plain.
Love yourself!
Respect yourself, hold Y-O-U in high esteem.
I dare you, I challenge you to show me *all*
that you can be.

Marlene Lewis
Brooklyn, NY

For the past sixteen years I have been educating young minds. As parents and certainly as educators, we experience the battle of the wills. In our world of technological advancement, our youth are wiser in terms of what they're exposed to, but weaker regarding the elements that they must overcome. "Hoochiemama Queen" speaks to the core, the spirit and the sensibilities of a student whom I was initially unable to reach because she was rebelling against authority. I was appealing for her to stand up, separate herself from negativity and allow her mind and character to develop to its full potential. I was challenging her to be all that she could be! This student developed mentally as well as emotionally. By the end of the school year, she was a different person. I would say, she rose up the way I challenged her, to become a young lady and not a street girl. I'm happy to say "Hoochiemama Queen" was a catalyst in that process!

My Beautiful Sarah

Let's keep our secret,
   You may not say words or speak the way others do,
But we understand each other,
   For that we know is true!
Your funny smile and your eyes ... that are so bright,
   Fill up my heart with a very special light.
I promise that day will come and we will meet,
   It will be on a golden shiny street.
We will throw our arms around each other,
   We'll both begin to cry,
Our tears will glow like a shiny star.
   That day I will call you,
"My beautiful Sarah," and you will say,
   "Hi Grandma."

Rita C. Dorney
El Paso, TX

Hero

He doesn't wear a cape and he never flies
But I see the magic and wonder in his eyes.
He's there when I need him, day or night
But he never assumes he's always right.
    He's my hero

He talks softly and doesn't say too much
But when he speaks my heart is touched.
He reads many books but doesn't know it all
But his faith in God makes him ten feet tall.
    He's my hero

He tells me great stories of long ago years
But always with a smile and never with tears.
He'll tell a joke or sometimes a funny line
But his love is always true and so is mine.
    He's my hero

He sees all the good beyond all the bad
But he's more than a hero, he's my Dad.

Linda Hewes
Easthampton, MA

Stallion in the Sky

The Holy Spirit flung the light of the morning sun upon my darkest hour
Lift up your head while you are praying beneath the trees, he said
Look up—look high—do not be denied
The clouds opened as if they were drapes upon a stage
See the stallion in the sky
Raised up on his hind legs his body bursting with bulging muscles
    everywhere
White upon white and his mane was long, wild and flowing in the
    current of air
Enlightenment pierced my soul when he turned and looked at me with
his
    diamond eyes
What delight occupied my soul from this once-in-a-lifetime white knight
A magical moment in time when time stood still
And the essence of his presence moved my heart to heal!

Alisha Beauchamp-Boettger
New Braunfels, TX

*Back in 1950, I was born in McCamey a little "oil boom town" in West
Texas. We had a life of hard times and great times. My five sisters and one
brother were raised by our father, the best old cowboy in Texas. I now live
in the beautiful awe-inspiring Texas Hill Country with my husband Robert
Boettger. Poetry is great therapy and I am very thankful and grateful when I
am inspired to write.*

This Is the End

I don't understand, I think too much,
I need to be alone and get off this crutch.
Focus is what I'm not good at,
Art is what screams to me,
My dreams are no longer reality and there's no room for insanity.
Take it as it is,
Read it as it's written,
For all that I know is I'm sailing away on a boat of confusion.
The boat sails away on the tears I've cried for days;
One day I'll reach the land to part with what could have been,
To never love you again.

Heather Nickey
Rocklin, CA

Music in the Wind

Music all around
music in your ear
what a wonderful sound
that you will hear.

When it passes by
and goes another way
I will wave good-bye
until another day.

Birdie L. Munoz
Atta Loma, CA

Serenity

The beauty of the endless ocean is free.
Watching waves waft against the wharf,
turmoil surrenders to the ubiquitous sea.
Breakers morph from towering to dwarf.

Watching waves waft against the wharf,
looking for tranquility away from the city.
Breakers morph from towering to dwarf,
seeing seamless seas searching for serenity.

Looking for tranquility away from the city,
providing solace and solitude from strife.
Seeing seamless seas searching for serenity,
a home to diverse plant life and wild life.

Providing solace and solitude from strife.
Clouds change their hue from blue to gray.
A home to diverse plant life and wild life,
a place for seal, dolphin and ray to play.

Looking for tranquility away from the city.
Turmoil surrenders to the ubiquitous sea,
seeing seamless seas searching for serenity.
The beauty of the endless ocean is free.

Gordon Bangert
Vail, AZ

Special Guests

You know, I have to tell you
About the guests I had today.
There were about a dozen of them
All dressed in black array.
They came for a special happening.
Don't think they've been here before.
They flew right in and landed ...
I could see and hear them from my door.
During the early morning hours
There had been an animal hit by a car.
As its body lay there in the sun awhile,
My guests could see and smell it from afar.
They flew right in and landed.
Their wonderful service began.
They worked all day cleaning it up
As if an EPA team were in command!
When a big truck drove by their site
They all flew to perch in a leafless tree.
Now that was a spooky sight to see!

Molly Randall
Oakland, MS

Living out in the "boondocks" of NW Mississippi, I see and experience much of what Mother Nature has to offer. There are lots of deer, hummingbirds, skunks, armadillos, and so many more. This particular morning I thought a deer had been hit by a car, as I saw my "Special Guests" arriving. It was not a deer but a very large dog that was killed by a passing car, and my "Special Guests" worked tirelessly to successfully clean up the mess.

If You Must

I you must leave me,
Leave me now
Before I awake to love's embrace

If you must leave me,
Leave me now
Before I sing the lover's song

If you must leave me,
Leave me now
Before you drink the ecstasy
From my lips
And bathe in the shower of mine eyes

If you must leave me,
Leave me now
Or stay eternally
Mine and none other—
Thus, said the flower to the bumble bee

Brigitte Cunning
Yonkers, NY

Thunder Drum Angel Band

Different kinds of drums, cymbals, cowbell and sticks,
Maracas
Our angels are putting on a concert for you
To let you know they're thinking of you,
Playing thunder drum music so you won't feel
So blue and to give you a rainbow from their
Thundershower too

Dorothy Ann Harris Moy
Grosse Pointe Park, MI

I am Dorothy Harris Moy from Grosse Pointe Park, MI. It is nice to be able to put a thought, inspiration or viewpoint into a verse, saying or poem. Writing is a good form of expression. The poem "Thunder Drum Angel Band" was inspired by Dan Hall, and is dedicated to Dan Hall, Bill Carlin, and Joel Lechner. Grosse Pointe South '76–2013 Angels.

Summer Solstice

Feathers of air whisper
Palm fronds shiver in delight
Long gone now, memories of
Yesterdays' cool nights

Dreams of golden times
Ride soft carpets of warmth
Flowers nod beguilingly
Mystically painting life

Bewitching scent of
Coconut perfumes
Speak tongues
Only goddesses understand

Bronzed muscles ripple
Silent sensuous reply
Sun-drenched skin reflects
Ribbon lines in oil

Scantly adorned worshippers
Savor summer solstice
With visions of love
Longing to be found

Joylin Mahl
Palm Desert, CA

Sunny summer days on a warm California beach are filled with glorious magic. Sunshine, warm sand and smiles fill the tropical air. Beautiful people, laughing children and even Grandma and Grandpa lying on colorful blankets are drawn here. Sweet memories! This balmy, delightful time was the inspiration for my poem. Latin sol (sun) and sister (stand still) thus Summer Solstice occurs on the longest day of summer. Wonderful things might happen! I was blessed to spend many years and many hours near the beach—Laguna Beach, Dana Point, Newport Beach, Huntington Beach, and many others. Now living in the desert, it all becomes a dream. Summer is mystical. Raising children in sunny California offers me a setting for many poems penned about the sea and people as well as mountains and deserts in verse.

Nature Calling

The sycamore tree shades me from the hot glaring sun's rays;
The midsummer's warmth wraps me into an afternoon gaze.

A little brown wren stops by to give an inquisitive glance;
So small and full of life it flutters off from its stance.

A pair of dragonflies dance through the breeze-blown air,
Hunting down their prey with a flamboyant flair.

Green blades of grass poking up between my toes;
And across the top of my foot a tiny red ant goes.

A young speckled robin perched above greets me with a chirp;
Minding my manners I hold back a burp.

Munching on clover the brown cottontail slowly will hop,
Grazing across my lawn to a cooler, shady spot.

Cardinals, finches and doves serenade as jays and crows scold;
Surrounded in my personal auditorium the feathered concerts unfold.

Oh, give thanks to the Lord, for yes He is good!
His creation surrounds me, I marvel where He once stood.

With a spirit-filled thanks I admire His works;
All the sights and sounds are His signature scripted with quirks.

Yes, a lazy Saturday afternoon, in my backyard there's so much to see;
Man, I just wish I didn't have to get up from this chair to go pee ...

David Davis
Woodstock, IL

A Mother's Love

My love for you will never die
No matter how many times you make me cry.
I carried you for nine months inside of me
Now I will carry you forever in my heart.
You grew from my baby girl to
A wife and a mother. You are like no other
I am proud to be your mother.
With all my love till the
End of time and beyond.

Margaret Rollins
Rochester, NH

*My beautiful daughters, Alice, Becky, and Shana are what inspired my poem,
"A Mother's Love." They are my world as well as my grandchildren and my
beautiful great-granddaughter. I love to write poetry and even songs. I have
two songs on CDs and another one to be recorded. I love doing crafts. I
might not have done much of what I do if it wasn't for my fiancé Ronnie. He
told me that I was good at things and that I could sing. He loved my singing.
He passed away December 19, 2011, and I owe all this to him. I am proud
to be a mother, grandmother, and great-grandmother. They have made my
life better.*

Madness

How many times must madmen go mad
Before we react to their crimes?
When do we stop being just sad
As our children's blood runs at prime time?

How many times must we sit and watch
The money-thieves steal our lives?
When do we stop listening to our politicians' lies
After they bargain with the lobbyists' prize?

How many times will we allow it to be said
That it's all someone else's fault?
How many times must madmen go mad
Before we react to their crimes?

Years come and go
Bullets fly—well we know.
Hitting innocents sitting like ducks in a row
How many years must madmen go mad?

Humankind can put a man on the moon, but
They cannot stop a madman in Syria, Aurora, or Rangoon.
Mankind can cruise over eight miles on Mars
While people starve by the thousands on Earth.

There is no answer—no not blowing in the wind
To how many times madmen must go mad
Before our world becomes sane.
For the answer lies within you and me.

Jacqueline Sue
Greenbrae, CA

Jacqueline Annette Sue's first book of poetry Morning Glories in a Dead Tree *was published in 2007. The poem "Madness" (2013) was written as protest to gun violence. Her other books are* A Dream Begun So Long Ago: The Story of David Johnson, Ansel Adams First African American Student *(2012);* Cornbread and Dim Sum *(2004);* Black Seeds in the Blue Grass *(1984) and the play* Mothers-in-Law in Vietnam *(2007). She is a San Francisco State University graduate with a master's degree from San Francisco Theological Seminary in San Anselmo, CA, and is married to documentary photographer David Johnson. Her website is www.jacquelinesue.com.*

Generations

Generations come and go.
Traditions ebb and flow.
The ultimate quest remains unchanged.
But how we attain it gets rearranged.
It's neither for better nor for worst.
We simply juggle what comes first.
My generation got lost in translation.
All morals devoured by attorneys' summations.
We spin the truth to suit the maker.
We crush the decent and celebrate the taker.
We do things because we can and not because we should.
Our actions are self-absorbed and defy the common good.
Antiquity tires of hubris as generations have told.
So I asked my daughter of twenty-one years what her generation would
    hold.
With a wink and a grin she began her tale of strength, courage and heart.
But a frown and a sigh replaced her reply when she got to the
    disappointing part.
Her generation she said was created and fed on insecurity, fear and greed.
Her father succumbed, her mother endured and what she discovered was
    need.
For her generation's hopes and dreams are vast yet strangely uncertain.
Family ties are there awkwardly beyond repair and examined as if through
    a curtain.
Morals are a fright, wrong is the new right and attorneys have guaranteed
    a battle.
Heroes are now zeros and legends are lost and technology leads us like cattle.
Still she is certain that she will prevail for something she has that I haven't.
An abundant supply of strength undefined which is locked in her
generational cabinet.
Generations remain the same yet each is altered.
They astonish and amaze but each has faltered.
Yet they remain the gift that keeps on giving
and are the traditions that make life worth living.

Julie Stack
Poway, CA

*My inspiration for this poignant poem was my ex-husband, an attorney
and an addict. His hubris shattered many lives and altered our generational
course, forever.*

Untitled

I was asked a question by a friend today
Who was thinking of retirement
He is approaching the age of sixty-five
And wants to know what he should do

Why he thought of me I do not know
Although I am retired
I continued my work twenty-four years beyond sixty-five
And could have gone more if I wanted

My designation was accountant
My specialty was taxes
My friend's work is akin to mine
Which is why he supposed that I would know

Retirement is a personal decision
There is no right or wrong
For me to go 'til eighty-nine was no big deal
But to you that might be wrong

The change from working to resting
Is fraught with problems galore
So many things are different
From what they were before

Make sure before you sign the papers
That you have thought things through
That you will have something solid
That you will like to do

Mel Gofstein
Phoenix, AZ

Mel is a ninety-year-young, retired tax accountant. His first poem was written in his mid-eighty-ninth year, just prior to his retirement. He has eighty poems with subjects from A to Z on hand as of now. His friends think they are pretty good. He has no known enemies. He is still writing.

The Dream

I traced your face with my fingers
In hopes you would feel my touch.
I whispered soft words in your direction,
Wishing them to reach your ears.
I dreamed I was walking beside you,
And you tenderly held my hand.
I longed for the words you could not speak,
For you were looking to another direction.
I stood in the shadows, alone, but filled
With a love that once was not to be.

Maryilyn Jessee
Moline, IL

"The Dream" was inspired because of an event that happened over forty years ago. The 45th class reunion was in 2012, and I had the fortunate experience of connecting with him, my first love. He was never aware of my feelings and I regret not having spoken up. As life often repeats, I again lost contact with him, but not my feelings. In place of a love song I wrote a poem. I also made a wish that he would find me and make a change to my ending, just as only he could take away my breathtaking air.

Waves

Waves are the heartbeat
Of the sea,
Rhythmically pounding
The shore
Then retreating,
In an endless cycle
Unceasing
Since time began.

Waves
That course through man,
Sustaining life,
Are vital
But puny in comparison
And finite
For man's heart
Beats for a moment
And is still.

While the sea,
The infinite sea,
That was present
At man's creation
Never pauses
In its ebb and flow
To note man's passing.

Beverly B. MacCallum
Pomona, CA

Dodging the Bus

What's there to discuss:
Promises shattered?
Lies hang around us,
Hopes *lie* dashed and splattered.

Promises shattered
Shot by blunderbuss
Hopes lie dashed and splattered,
Told, "Don't make a fuss,"

Blasted by blunderbuss
I stumble, tattered,
Told, "Don't make a fuss,"
My blood, spattered,

I stumble, tattered,
Dodge the bus!
My blood ... spattered,
No time to cuss.

Dodge the bus?
So broken, battered,
No time to cuss,
My thoughts have ... scattered,

So broken, battered,
Lies hang us!
My thoughts have ...
What's there to discuss?

Keenan Woods
San Diego, CA

The pantoum was originally titled "Phantoum Pantoum" before it evolved into a darker, more serious poem. In "Dodging the Bus," the author comments on abusive relationships and their prisoners. Keenan Woods is a chemist by training and a writer at heart. He recently graduated from California Lutheran University with a BS in chemistry and a minor in English. He is currently pursuing his PhD in chemistry at the University of Oregon. Woods hopes to teach organic chemistry at a university and to publish a fantasy novel. He would like to thank his family, girlfriend, and professors for their support.

My Patient

I wonder if he's going to make it through the night!
It's all in God's hands if he gives up his fight.
He's all alone—the nurse and he
His family is all gone—wherever they may be.
His breath—I'm wondering—which will be his last?
The pulse is so slow—before it was fast.
She moves him about from side to side
To break down now would be his demise.
His pressure is dropping minute by minute
I know this man is not going to win it.
Not long ago he was a big hunk of a man
His body has withered—he is holding God's hand.
This man so valiantly fought for his life
I know he just went through all sorts of strife.
I wonder what the man would have to say
If he knew that on this earth it was his last day.
How does one give up and lie motionless
Waiting to go to a life of bliss?
You sort of envy this man now that he's gone
To think, "No more pain," now that he's reached the dawn.

Rita M. Krieger
Ponte Vedra, FL

I am a registered nurse and was doing private duty nursing at this hospital in Pennsylvania. This patient of mine was just in and out of it (fighting for his life) for days but finally lost the battle. I just had to write about him. This is just one of the patients I will always remember. I am eighty-three years of age—don't feel it, act it, or look it. I have six children and seventeen grandchildren. I am very, very busy.

Kindred Spirit

Every once in a while, as we travel along,
Our appointed succession of days,
We chance on a soul, with whom we're attuned,
And it seems we have known them always.

There is instant appeal in the warmth of their smile,
And a sparkle of joy in their eyes;
You find much in common, each subject you share,
While conversing, the time simply flies!

Like a foretaste of Heaven, where everyone's kin,
In the wonderful family of God;
Being helpful not harmful, in all that we do,
While sojourning here on this sod.

So be alert and aware, of all that's around,
A true zest for living, display;
It might lift the spirits of someone you meet,
And could guide them in finding their way.

For opportunity's there, to learn and to grow,
From the beginning of life, to its end;
In exchanging ideas and thoughts with another,
You may find you have made a new friend.

But the best of all knowledge, that one can impart,
Are those blessings, which come from above;
Through the beautiful Savior, who died in our place,
Perfect proof of God's mercy and love.

Eleanor Lau
San Marcos, CA

Poetry Is ...

The expression of one's soul
Poetry is my inner home
I rely on it to stay sane
I turn to it when I'm drained
For me it is my savior
It's a friend who does favor after favor
To learn more about me from each word I write
When I reread them in the daylight
Nighttime is my time to confess
In my notebook I try to sort out the mess
All too confusing when circling in my mind
The thoughts come out nice and simple and
I'm surprised at what I find
You would be too, if you just took a minute
To reach deep within and listen to it
Listen to your inner voice
It will provide you with the right choice

Marissa Alexandria McLeod
Ripon, CA

Peace

You gave me hope,
When I found none;
When I lost my way,
Felt all undone.
The past no longer
causes pain or loss;
I've found out something
More to know—to gain.
I never counted the cost,
It's here below I've learned,
There was mounted
A plan to open wide
The great life of love;
Of hope, of healing from above.
It's in your leading
There is no fear.
For in Your arms I am blessed,
With calm like a quiet cove,
And coo of a gentle dove,
Your thoughts whisper peace.

Darlene Stewart
Independence, MO

Reflections

I reached a most reflective stage
When first I could recall
My father when he was my age.
How mem'ries did enthrall!

For I compared his life before
With mine, rememb'ring what
He loved and feared—and ev'ry door
He opened, each he shut.

Then reflection shone ahead because
I knew that my child would
Recall me at the age I was—
And my actions, bad and good.

I felt a heightened urgency
To share life's full carafe—
A new responsibility
To lead, to love, to laugh.

Now I myself rededicate,
As time and truth advance,
To live as morals indicate—
By choice and not by chance.

And yet I know when we look through
Time's windows near and far,
Reflection is not just what we do;
It's partly who we are.

Kenneth Trobaugh
St. Simons Island, GA

The Poem

Words come easy
when they impart
the thoughts in the brain
that come straight from the heart.

No matter the subject,
or to whom or what the words pertain,
once the words are on paper
it's a special title they became.

Sometimes funny
and sometimes serious,
and sometimes a mixture of both;
but whatever the concoction,
it's words that deliver the most.

Just read it one line at a time
and when the last line is read,
look back and know
you really liked what it said.

Hope Antoniadis
Jacksonville, FL

Our Goddess, Sophia Adored

I stood by my window
Looking into the afternoon sun;
I found Sophia lighted by its rays
Totally, brilliantly
Beckoning all to her attention.

Sophia stood tall, determined, wise
Holding at her side the olive branch, always
Surrounded in spirit by her handmaidens
Peace and love, justice and truth—
All close companions wherever we find her.

Suddenly these western rays dimmed;
In the fast-sinking sun,
Sophia appeared cold, shivering.
Instead of being totally shining,
I found her gray, darkening.

A shimmering shawl
Did little to keep her warm.
Still, with one breast showing
Reminding onlookers, she nurtures
All in the world who seek this lady of wisdom.

Donald R. Eldred
Jacksonville, IL

I started writing when I was nine years old sitting at my grandma's kitchen table while the old folks were conversing in the parlor. After college and university I spent some fifty-plus years as a teacher of writing and literature. During several autumn and summer terms I studied at Worcester College and Christ Church College of Oxford University in England. My major covocation was Thomas Hardy. My very first published poem was in the Hardy Society Journal *in 2007. I retired from the classroom in 2006 and spent considerable time writing. For the past ten years I have been a regular visitor at Gladstone Library, a residential academy and spiritual retreat center in North Wales, UK. The poem "Our Goddess, Sophia Adored" I wrote in 2012. My room has always been #10, both windows looking out at the Statue.*

The Truth about Society

Society is a rabid beast
Like a vast creature of the unknown
Like a bottomless chamber of many secrets
Like a dim mask that may never be shown

Society is a rotting beast
Demons to be unleashed
By the cold and ghastly wrath of the social media
Beguiling to be released

Society is a mendacious beast
A book of endless lies
A story based on judgments
Wrecking our delicate human eyes

Society is a murderous beast
One by one by one
Slowly twisting our shattered minds
Like rotten, rusty, creaking doorknobs
Forever trapping us inside

Society is doing no harm
Just slowly devouring away
And our brain, our heart, our body, our soul
Will no longer be here to stay

Society simply severs our softened silenced soul
After longing for a needed sleep
But sleep there is no time for
When all our sore and tired eyes can do is weep

Isabella Scaffidi
Mequon, WI

*A lot of people ask me what inspired my poem "The Truth About Society."
And while there really was no clear, certain answer, I could come up with
this: The poem was written because of what I've learned while being a
teenage girl in today's society, that those models and pictures we see practically
everywhere we look are illusions. That girl you saw in that magazine doesn't
even look like that girl in the magazine. Makeup, Photoshop, all of it tricks us,
making us feel ugly, because we don't look like those models. All of it is lies.*

Rossie Baseball

Harry Adams loved baseball through and through.
And all the other Rossie ballplayers loved it too.
Time was always made for the games to be played,
On Rossie's diamond and in many another town,
Playing hard each year to take the crown.
Tam Black was their coach and knew all the ways,
To make it a great game with all of the plays.
Pitching a no-hitter and catching fly balls,
Hitting a home run was the best of all.
And oh, for the lights so they could play games at night.
They had such good times and pleased the crowd,
Who kept cheering for more,
Oh so loud.
Many years flew by but it didn't seem long,
Til their age gave way to not being as strong.
And so finally it was time to hang up their gear,
To give up the fun of yesteryear.
But oh, what memories those years recall,
Of all the great times of Rossie Baseball.

Naomi Adams
Milford, IA

I am ninety years old, and this is my first time entering a poetry contest. I wrote it because of my husband, Harry, and his Rossie teammates' love of baseball. He played all four years in high school, the only freshman to make the team, and many years on the Rossie Town Team as a pitcher and an outfielder. He died two years ago after a long farming career. My children and grandchildren are proud of me for writing this poem. We were blessed with a wonderful husband, father, and grandfather.

One of the Pieces of Life

It's funny how a stranger can be an important piece
To the biggest puzzle called life, which proves to be bittersweet.

You came and stole my heart away, you're now my personal thief.
But you gave me more than you ever took, which is hard for me to believe.

Little did we know, that a short three years ago, you were nothing but a
name.
But here we stand, comprehending what we can, realizing our lives will
never be the same.

I gave you my trust, my love, everything I could.
Until one day, you turned away, and did something you swore you never
would.

I feel crushed, I feel alone, I've become a complete wreck.
It's too sudden, I can't breathe with the hands of agony around my neck.

Should I feel pain? Anger? I'm at a loss for what to do with my mind.
Do I seek revenge? Comfort? Perhaps all that can heal me is time.

Time. It goes by slowly as my happiness fades.
Day by day, hour by hour, I wonder who you became.

But here come the regrets, the sorrows, the surprises coming from you.
The lies, the suffering, the pain you caused, the dreadful days you rue.

I should leave, I shouldn't listen, you said what you had to say.
But I'm too forgiving, the second chance is there, I can't be the one that
got away.

So here we are, round two, and you're back to the stranger you once
were.
Gentle, caring, kind and jubilant, to my despair you were the cure.

Regarding the fact that you were the cause of my sadness, you hold the
key to my heart once more.
While you help me with this part of the puzzle, the rest of the pieces
shall remain on the floor.

Allie McCallips
Durand, IL

Princess of the Sea

Would you like to be a princess of the sea,
or would you rather be, a little girl like me?
If I were a princess of the sea
Would I still look just like me?
Could my long and shining hair
float on water same as air?
Could I wear my ruffles and my bows,
or would I have a tail, instead of toes?
Would my eyes still open wide
even when I had to dive?
Could I smell a flower fair
or hug a cuddly teddy bear?
Could I pick an apple from a tree
or watch a buzzing bumble bee?
Could I run and dance and play
and see the sunset every day?
Could I go high up in my swing
or chase a butterfly and sing?
Is the shining, great big blue sea,
or the pretty green grass most fun for me?
I think when my bright and pretty day is done,
and the dark night time starts to come,
A little girl just like me
is just exactly what I want to be ...

Jackie Bryant
Murray, UT

Silence

In the cold depths of the night
disappearing deeper and deeper
into the recesses of my mind
and dreaming of the dead as if
their secrets could be revealed

Behind the walls of my eyelids
I retreat from the stormy skies to be
carried by the unforgiving arms of the ocean
to a forever paradise inside my mind
where the stars fade, but I linger on.

Teetering between the line of dream and reality
where everything has its price.
I stand alone, looking up for the signs
in the darkened silence that is all consuming.
Silence is all I've become
and I've found a place to rest my head.

Braley Quall
Melrose, WI

9/11

On September 11, 2001, Al-Qaeda-like terrorists made headlines in a very dramatic way.

Not the Joint Chiefs of Staff, not the CIA, no Americans were prepared for the events of that day!

Continuing their plans, those nineteen terrorists separated into four groups each known as a cell.

They boarded planes in Boston, New Jersey and D.C.—headed for sites Americans know very well.

Flights 11 and 175 were hijacked by cells numbers one and two.

At 8:45 then, at 9:06—those jets did the jobs they were piloted to do.

New York's Twin Towers were rammed with a deafening sound!

Those well-known landmarks began crumbling to the ground.

It is now 9:40 A.M.—and at a place near our nation's Capitol in Washington, D.C.

Horrified Americans were about to learn the sinister deed of cell number three.

Those diabolical demons struck the very core of our military's might.

They crashed Flight 77 into the Pentagon—what a troubling sight!

As we watched television, we were gripped with fear.

Would those terrorists destroy this land that we love so dear?

Please, someone please tell us, please—how in the world could any of this be?

What was happening to this land that means so much to you and to me?

It was 10:37 A.M. disquieted Americans heard that the fourth cell had struck.

Thankfully, three Americans on that jet overpowered the terrorists— dashing their luck!

Instead of being rammed into a revered, historical building in Washington, D.C.

A boggy field in Shanksville, Pennsylvania became the entombment for Flight 93.

At long last the mind-boggling, body-numbing, pyre is gone from each nightmare-evoking site.

The President, mayor, and others tell us at the end of the tunnel there is a bright light.

We know that wars, acts of terrorism, and natural disasters will come and go.

As Americans, we will stand tall and press on—this is what we want the whole world to know!

Odelle Edwards
Vallejo, CA

Shoes of Holocaust

Embedded under glass
in the flooring of Yad Vashem,
a crumpled shoe collection
tells the secrets of evil men gone mad.
Most are sturdy lace-ups
in scruffy shades of black or brown,
but some are dainty party shoes.
creamy-colored ballet slippers,
with satin ribbons curled
across leather darkness,
give an eerie elegance
to the crystal coffin of suffering.

The Nazi mementos
came off the German prisoners,
whose only crime was being a Jew.
The glassy grave in Jerusalem
holds the tears and silent screams
of innocence being shoved barefooted
into gas chambers at Auschwitz
and fiery ovens at Buchenwald.

Some ungodly men claim
the cruelty never happened,
but the sickening smoke of burning bodies
still circles the globe with wind,
and battered shoes off the feet of the dead
tell the horror stories of Holocaust.

Kitty Yeager
Arkadelphia, AR

Insomnia

Seeing four little numbers slowly change to three, barely separated by a
colon
The bed sheets tangled around your legs like seaweed
But instead of being dragged into the depths of sleep
Memories and treasure-chest-thoughts float up from the abyss of your
subconscious
Faces of the long-forgotten race to the mainstream of your thought \
process like bubbles
Popping at the surface and releasing the words that had been savagely
repressed
You feel like you're drowning, but not in the peaceful sense of sinking
into a dark comfort
Drowning as in the thrashing and desperate attempt to find any sort of
comfort
Drowning as in the thrashing and desperate attempt to find any sort of
comfort
Your throat swells and you try to blink with your paper eyelids over
encrusted glass eyeballs
Your mind moves like a train through quicksand
Part of it wants to go full steam ahead
While the other part of it is trying to slow down for a stop in the station
Only the dock you jumped off of earlier
And the train you're trapped on are all a part of the same God-forsaken
destination
Insomnia

Alyssa Larger
Menomoree Falls, WI

A Mother's Love

Having a son is the joy of my life,
but it can also be a big fight.
Rich is his name and he loves to play games.
I love to cheer, all through the year.
He was the class clown, the best kid in town.
He loves his mom with all his heart,
they will never be apart.
He's all grown up now, I couldn't
be more proud.
He moved away three years ago today.
When I see him again my
heart will be okay.

Mary Aeppli
Mesa, AZ

Summer Break

Listening to dangling chimes
We'll be sure to have good times
Splashing in the pool all day
Going to the pretty bay
Summer is a scorching time
Refreshing water with a lime
Enjoy your summer break
For goodness sake!

Kaitlyn Vierra
Attleboro, MA

Becoming

My God loved me this much
to see with eyes that such as
mine could not—
The way He planned for me ...
—to come to know Him—
He laid for me a plan
then held an outstretched hand
the way for me to go ...
—to come to trust Him—
The way is painfully slow—I
rush and stumble as I go
Rebelling against His perfect will
until exhausted—lying still ...
—I come to obey Him—
My life spins out before my face
as through His mercy—saved by grace
through faith
My Lord and Savior takes His place
within my heart ...
—to come to love him—
Our spirits joining now as one
as from my yes—He has begun
A healing change as I become ...
—like Jesus—

Carol Wilkinson
Cornwall, NY

*I feel honored to join you in that enticing—sometimes secretive—space
where poets venture to bring forth their notations. Regarding the contest— I
decided to follow the advice of my pastor and friends and enter. My writings
began about age twelve—now in middle age—and are mostly personal,
usually about what was taking place in my life at that time. My goal when
I write is to try to express my deep feelings that I'm unable to reveal other
ways. I give all praise to God for blessing me with this gift I share with you.*

6A

Read today on 6A
Soldier killed
First of year
Afghanistan

Interred in
Arlington
Where others lie
Who died fighting for the
US of A

Sisters mourn
Mother's given a flag
Remembrance

Bravery
Sacrifice

Oh what would
That soldier have done
If he had lived to
Twenty-one?

Fred W. Reichenbach
Lehighton, PA

Fred Reichernbach began writing poetry in 2008 with a focus on existentialism, good versus evil, and human interactions. The author of the novel and a collection of short stories, both yet to be published, he is a director of consultants at a software company. He resides with his wife, Toni, in Lehighton, Franklin Township, PA and is a father to three daughters.

This Tangled Ryegrass Maze

Back then, when a last veil of burning lay
Upon brown laminated hills, and leaves
Were yet unloosed, as yet undead, the day
Hung suspended, much like an unmoored fluff.
Of thistledown, caught up in churning air.
Yet, in the moment that the first leaf fell,
We knew that such unfinished things were there—
As summer haze, and tears, and wilted buds
That died unnoticed in the tangled ryegrass maze.
Back then, when fog banks swelled upon the rise,
As harbingers of changing wind, the fringe
Of seed pods at the fence row line, to cries
Of waning summer warmth, remained unclaimed
As castoffs of the summer breeze, confused
Within the colder pull of wind-caught autumn skies.
In shadow now, the place remains, where we
Once gathered seed lint to the mournful slough
Of wind in cottonwoods. We knew the sea
Of grass between the fieldstone and the fog
To be unreachable. Yet, years dissolved
Into these soft impatient hills, and tears
Fell down, remembered, in this tangled ryegrass maze.
Goodbyes were never spoken, only felt.

Maggie McGuire
Wiota, IA

A retired registered nurse in emergency/trauma nursing, Reverend Maggie is a very busy retiree. A resident of rural Iowa, Maggie's writing is a natural outflow of the beauty that is her heritage, an expression of the peaceful world that surrounds her. She is an artist with numerous oil paintings hanging everywhere in her house. She has had multiple nursing articles published in Supervisor Nurse Magazine, *plus* RN Magazine; *one fiction novel,* Wind Stalker, *about an Irish Setter dog lost in Oregon, finding his way home to Iowa. Poetry has been a lifetime endeavor, hobby and passion, with some published in local newspapers, and, more recently, in* Timeless Voices (2005), The Best Poems and Poets of 2007, *and* Today's Best Poets (2013). *Back around 1969 Maggie was named Poet Laureate of Washington State Federated Clubs. Most importantly, reverend McGuire is an ordained minister of the gospel of Christ, having been "saved" late in life and called into a ministry of evangelism. She continues in evangelistic outreach, also producing "Lamp on a Hill" radio ministry on a local secular radio station. Two wonderful companion dogs, Golden Retrievers, Buddy and Hud, share the quiet life in a farm country.*

Mother's Garden

My mother loved the flowers
Each season brought new blooms.
With joy she would plant and till and weed.
It chased away her glooms.

She knew the names of all she tended,
She was a master of her trade.
Her hands were strong and knew no wrong,
They were the best God ever made.

She tried to teach me all she knew,
But little then did I care.
For if I needed flowers, I thought
My mother would always be there.

My mother loved her garden,
'Til Heaven she did go.

And I now tend the flowers;
With a love that is real and true.
For when I'm in my garden, Mom,
I am closest there to you.

Janice Nokes
Lebanon, TN

I have been married forty-nine years to a retired military man of thirty years. We live on a small farm with horses, pygmy goats, bees, and birds. I have two children, a son and daughter and five grandchildren. I was inspired to write this poem on "Mother's Day," while reminiscing all the wonderful times my mother and I shared together, while she was living. She was the best ever. There is no love like a mother's love.

Born to Fly

I'm just a girl who was born to fly,
to lift off the earth and soar the sky.
I've looked down to the birds and up to God's feet;
I've spun, I've flipped,
and through the clouds I zipped;
I've felt freedom in its purest form.
I earned my silver wings, and they are proudly worn.
To you I'm a hero, I've paved the way;
But to myself, I'm a girl who was just born to fly,
to lift off the earth, and soar the sky.
It was love at first flight, and I'll never forget my first landing!
The excitement, the anxiety, the rush, it was outstanding!
Thank you for saluting me, thank you for your praise.
And the Congressional Gold Medal ... wow! I don't even know what to
    say.
I've lived my life to the fullest, I followed my dreams,
I've inspired many, unintentionally.
But I'm just a girl that was born to fly,
to lift off the earth and soar through the sky ...

Carolyn R. Farmer
Shillington, PA

*I've always looked up to my aunt Kay, who will be ninety this January. Her
stories about her love of flying have always inspired me. You see, she was a
member of the Women's Air Force Service Pilots (WASP) during WWII,
which later earned her the highest of military honors. Recently she was at
her WASP reunion where they allowed her to take a plane up and fly! I was
looking at side by side pictures of her flying, one from today and one from
sixty-nine years ago! I just had to write this for her!*

Lamentation

I was as tall as she
Watching Mother trudge through deep snow
Take a taxi, fly to Reno,
Freedom from Father, Sister and me.

She went away, did not return
To the husband who beat her.
I got it, I understood,
Yet only eleven years old.

Did not anyone notice
My friends took care of me.

Joan Adams
Montcair, NJ

Lovers' Eyes

You say you see me with a full head of hair
even though
we both know,
like the emperor's new clothes
there's nothing there.
I trace the outline of your young-girl figure
but when you look at yourself in the mirror
you view the reflection of another
perhaps someone resembling your mother.
We have come to see each other
through aging's disguise
with the clearer vision
of lovers' eyes ...

James Fly
Amazonia, MO

James Fly earned his B.A. in journalism from Pacific Union College in Angwin, CA. He has edited church and college publications as well as two weekly newspapers. His children's book, Africa Adopted Us, *is currently being reprinted by the Pacific Press. An avid photographer, he belongs to the Midwest Artists Association and was a founding member of a Gallery 7, a former cooperative art gallery in downtown St. Joseph, MO. "Lovers' Eyes" was inspired by a statement made one morning by his wife, Constance R. Saxton.*

Happy Fall

The long, hot summer is nearly past.
Fall is just around the corner at last.
As I go walking through the trees,
I feel a gentle, chilling breeze.
The brightly colored leaves fall gently to the ground.
The squirrels are as busy as little bees scurrying around
filling their cheeks 'til they can hold no more;
gathering nuts for their winter's store.
Seasons come and seasons go
as nature puts on her fabulous show.
But, fall is my favorite time of year;
a time of change, a time of cheer.
Once again it's nature's call.
Happy fall to one and all.

Betty Arnold
Whittier, NC

As far back in my life as I can remember, I have been a lover of nature, of all God's wonderful creations, such as animals, birds, mountains, beautiful scenery, etc. Since my husband and I moved to the beautiful Smoky Mountains of North Carolina several years ago, I can hardly wait for fall to come each year with the cooler temperatures and rich, vibrant colors of the leaves. It's such a beautiful season, my favorite time of year.

Thanks for the Bluebells

When the bluebells bloom along the Shenandoah,
Along the winding river road I love to roam,
As I walk along I talk with God our Father,
Giving thanks for all the seeds His hands have sown.

It seems a million seeds just floated down from Heaven
And landed softly here on Shenandoah's shore.
As they floated down they turned to bells of azure,
Sifting gently through the blue where angels soar.

There they picked up just a little touch of glory
That made them sparkle in the early morning sun.
So we mortals could see just a touch of Heaven,
And give our thanks and praise to God the Holy One.

I thank the Lord for all the geese, so gently gliding,
And for the birds, on blooming branches, as they sing.
It seems they're praising God for sending us the bluebells,
As they usher in the glorious days of spring.

A great blue heron stands on jutting rock before me,
And like a sentinel he guards the banks of blue.
It seems that God has placed him here as their protector,
as bluebells glisten through the sunlit morning dew.

In giant sycamores the squirrels play and frolic,
Majestic eagle watches closely for his prey.
Lord, I hope that we will never lose the passion,
To save the beauty You have shown us here today.

Ann H. Hudson
Berryville, VA

Stop the Time for You and I

Days go by as quick as that
I'll make a moment for you and I
with the sun on our faces
the time will last forever

Life can lead to many surprises
so we'll find a special time
to focus on you and I
no matter what happens to us

I'll always be in your heart
now and forever
so be mine for the time
we have together

Elise Miller
South Elgin, IL

I Am a Jew

For thousands of years I have been prosecuted, persecuted, beaten,
bludgeoned, burned, humiliated, harmed in so many ways—
for I am a Jew

Christians, Moslems, Romans, Germans, Russians, Poles, French,
Italians, Austrians, supremacists, on and on have had their time in history
of hate—
for I am a Jew

I have not coveted other lands, raped, pillaged, or hated in return.
Meekly I have permitted my fate—
for I am a Jew

I feel, love, have compassion, look, taste, bleed, hurt, wonder, plan,
think in the same way as all of those called mankind—
for I am a Jew

I ask not that anyone join in my beliefs, do not force, cajole, argue that
my way is the only way to salvation. I ask only to believe in peace—
for I am a Jew

For those leaders of low self-esteem, who need power over others and
always need a scapegoat, I am stubborn and refuse to be an endangered
species. For this I am hated and attacked—
for I am a Jew

I know not what crimes I have committed to bring such wrath and hate
over so many centuries, but enough is enough—I stand on Masada
in protest. I stand with the young Maccabees of today in proclaiming,
"Never Again"—
for I am a Jew

Bernard Freedlander
Framingham, MA

New-Mom Thoughts

How peaceful you sleep,
my babe in arms
The sleep of an infant secure
in your innocence
As I gaze at your pink
mouth and up-turned nose
It's amazing how quickly my
little child grows
A short time ago we were
one you and me
And then in an instant
your eyes opened to see
A young world, a small
world, a curious mind
A beautiful smile making
your mom's world sublime
And yet as I sit and
watch you in sleep
I wish I could stop time
and you close to me keep
This is not fair for
everyone grows
My mom told me what
every mom knows
First step, second step
third step—four
Soon you'll be tall
enough to open the door
And if you see a tear
in your mom's eye
It's because the world
is now yours I cry

Joyce Barton-Carman
Newington, CT

Life Poetry

I am from a big room
From watching videos on my Kindle, from sleeping on a comfy bed
And a closet full of nice clothes
I am in my perfect bedroom

I am from a big place
From a big kitchen, from chilling in the family room
And a playroom with a nice TV and Xbox
I am in my cozy, amazing house

I am from a fun place
From playing with friends, from nice green grass
And swimming in my pool
I am in my perfect neighborhood

I am from lots of love
From lots of caring, from sharing stuff
And loads of fun
I am part of a perfect family

I am from a free place
From a beautiful place, from a place where things are green
And a place with amazing states
I am in the amazing United States of America

I am from good education
From playing soccer, from having a family
And being rich not just with money but everything in life
I am talking about my future

Kevin Martin
Melville, NY

My Love

Here I sit, day by day, just thinking how you went away
Here I sigh, still wondering why, oh why you went away
Here I chatter, like a mad hatter since you went away
Here I will cry until the day I die, thinking about why you went away

So you see until the day you return there is nothing left inside to yearn
for your love has gone away ...

Melissa Ciesmelewski
Keansburg, NJ

Breaking Up Is Hard to Do ...

You hide your bills from me.
I ask you to show me the last
bill that went through on the computer,
you say, "No."
I walk away from you.
I tell you, "I want to be divorced
from you forever."
You go to the door to leave, I tell
you, "You will pay back the money you
stole from people."
I worry about your health
and call you to come home.
You don't come back.

Janie Jo Crowe
Silverdale, WA

The Iron Peach

Oh, how great the days of yesteryear. So full of youthful praise and promise. Bright blue skies, no clouds, clear green fields as far as the eye can peer. A giant sweet bite into a juicy red apple, confirmed my greatness within my very soul, never ever leaving a bitter taste in which to take its toll. Stiff inner body fortitude resting in my great contribution to this world and my kingdom seems never-ending, eternal, never touching my sinful soul. Fame and rich living deem me unstoppable, my mountain high so fine, not to be unfurled as my fellow man lies wounded, footprints I leave behind. Oh, count the cost you feeble; my fruits of labor bless me. This peach you now have given me, I savor juice divine, bite and chew forever till all is might and life's new fruits all mine. Hark! My mouth fails to penetrate the skin of said round. My jaws broke, my teeth crushed to the very root! Oh pain, oh pain now fills my narrow frame as clouds of wrath pour in. The tastes of the juicy red were now replaced with an iron peach of sin. Be gone, dark clouds of Satan, bring back my past delights. I can't enjoy this iron peach; I've lost my appetite.

George Peterson
Marlborough, CT

Mother: Losing a Loved One

It's been a year ago today
That the Lord called you away,
you went through the heavenly gates.
You are in our hearts everyday.

We miss you more, but I know
you are safe with the Lord.
I miss the things we used to do,
just me and you.
We talked about the good stuff
even the bad,
you were the best mother,
and grandmother we could
ever have.

I didn't want you to leave me,
but now I see:
for Lord, "You wanted it to be."
You were always by my side,
you were with me all the time.

They say it takes time
for our hearts to heal
but with your help Lord,
I hope it will: give Irene a kiss and a hug.
Tell her the family sends love.

Donna Couch
Collinsville, AL

My name is Donna Couch, and I live in Colbran—it's between Fort Payne and Collinsville, AL—with my husband, Jeff, and three pets. I have always been interested in poetry. I have a notebook full of poems. The words I put together on paper are how I feel inside. It comes from the heart. So in time I hope these words will be an inspiration for someone else like they have been for me. I thank God for giving me the ability to put words together that really mean something. Thank you for taking the time to read it. May God bless each and every one of you.

For Jim

Your gentle touch makes me happy
The tender way you hold my hand
The quiet way you love me
Took me years to understand.

We've shared the good times
And cried together too
I know that in this whole world
there is no other just like you.

You've seen me through my bad times
And give me strength to carry on
Knowing when I awake each morning
I will never be alone.

What a difference you've made
Bringing love into my life
You are living in my heart
And make me proud to be your wife.

I think about you everyday
You are my closest friend
Can't wait to see your smile
And travel life's journey to the end.

Judy M. Van Zile
Rittman, OH

A Savor Limerick

There once was a group known as "Savor"
Whose goal all its members did favor,
To share what delights in both verse and in prose,
And from this they never did waiver.

They met twice each month, right after lunch
Each to read what of interest he or she'd found,
Sometimes a poem or a quote or a rhyme.
It need not be something profound.

How nice to have something in common
A group that just loves to read,
To share what to each brings great pleasure
Turns out to be pleasure indeed.

Betty C. Bones
Pinole, CA

I am eighty-five years old and a resident of an independent living facility for seniors in Pinole, CA. There was no group or activity for readers when I entered Bay Park in 2000, and within a year or so I'd begun such a group which I called SAVOR. Share, Articles, Verses, Original creations, Readings of all kinds. In order to publicize the group I wrote my poem (a limerick, really) which was followed immediately by management's decision to include it in their "welcome bag" for new residents. In 2011 SAVOR celebrated its ten-year anniversary.

My World as a Stage

I see the world as a stage
With every day and time a new page
Every event tells a story, paints a picture in my mind.

If the world was a stage
I'd play the lead
Singing and dancing like no one's watching me
If you give me a chance, I could show you my world as a stage.

Every scene, another song
That makes me feel like I belong
Everything falls into place, like the missing puzzle piece I find.

If the world was a stage, I'd play the lead.
Singing and dancing like no one's watching me.
If you give me a chance, I could how you my world as a stage.

I'd picture myself alone in a meadow, spread my arms as if they were
    wings
I'd still feel small walking along the sea
With all those great times looking back at me.

Sometimes, I feel like a kid who dreams of making it big.
Like there's a passion inside me and I've just got to let it show.

If the world was a stage, I'd play the lead.
Singing and dancing like no one's watching me.
If you give me a chance, let me sing my song and do my dance,
I could show you my world as a stage.

My world as a stage, make it come to life.
Put on a show for everyone to know
What it's like to have
My world as a stage.

Helen Brown
Nashville, TN

One Day at a Time

Six little girls you have raised up to women,
one day at a time
Who wiped our noses when we were little
and held our hands when we were young.
Who gave us a bath and helped us with math
one day at a time

Who washed our socks and combed our hair
and taught us to share,
who made us biscuits and taught us to cook
and helped us read our books,
one day at a time

Who let us pull up a chair, to stand on and help,
and make a tent in the middle of the floor.
Mama did all this and more
one day at a time

Who made us popcorn balls and homemade ice cream
who let us run in the rain and play in the snow,
you know, our mama did of course.
We watched you Mama and you taught us how to be a
mother one day at a time

Carolyn Brown
Muscle Shoals, AL

*I'm a sixty-four-year-old Southern Lady, married fifty years to my high school
sweetheart, with two children and three grandchildren. I've always loved
reading poetry, but never tried writing until I retired. I usually write poems
as a way to say thank you or show my love, as with the one I sent in for
the contest. It was about my mother, for my mother on Mother's Day. The
words were all true and easy to write. I'm the oldest of six girls raised by a
stay-at-home mother, in a slower time, one day at a time.*

White Light

We are all in transit to a star
Coming and going like wisps in
A night of tears,
Beckoning the future,
Stepping forward

Gently folding the tips
Of angel's wings
That flutter in the light
At the portal
Of a dream, awaiting
The image that fades ...

Blades of grass that shrink
Into sheaves of ice
Molten in summer sunshafts,
Bathing the earth in the
Liquor of their verdant beings,

To pass silently into the darkness,
And in blessed disbelief
We enter the light

To smolder on the edge of
Consciousness, awakening after
Millennia of slumber,
From a reverie of life,
To the light beyond
In transit to a star.

Ann Ilton
Boca Raton, FL

The transient nature of our lives and the swift passage of time inspired my poem. After a great tragedy struck there have been glorious miracles of hope. I am seventy-five and have worked as a teacher, a college administrator and a librarian among other pursuits. At one point I realized that a radiant light is there if we just recognize it and see with our inner eye. As a wife, friend, parent, and grandparent my goal is to transcend the illusions of despair, embrace hope and bring it to others. Thus, among my works of poetry is "White Light."

Wishing Upon a Star

Love is like an endless roller coaster,
Fluttering butterflies in my belly,
Admiring your dark brown eyes twinkling in the light.
Wanting to get to know you more,
But, "afraid" of rejection.
Thinking of you from time to time.
Now knowing anything about you except your name,
And wearing plaid shirts and khaki pants each day.
You seem so dreamy like a "shining star"
Just wanting to get to know you more.
But, "afraid" of rejection.
I keep quiet hiding in my shell like a snail.

Danielle Sparacio
Centereach, NY

Danielle Sparacio lives in Long Island, NY. She is a memoir writer, artist, and was a daycare teacher. She earned a bachelor's degree in both art education and fine arts. Currently, she is working for a well-known company on Long Island in another field. Sparacio is taking care of her son who has been diagnosed with Attention Deficit Hyperactive Disorder (ADHD) and Mood Disorder. She's a devoted mother to her son who's sports-oriented and a straight-A student. Sparacio wrote the poem "Wishing Upon a Star" based on a guy she likes but does not know.

Love Is Forever

You are strong, I am strong
And together we can't go wrong.
You are the one that I love.
You are my gift sent from Heaven above.
You are my amazing grace.
I am always delighted to see your face.
I am very happy that you are mine.
With you I always feel fine.
You give me a natural high.
My love for you will never die.
You are my eternal friend.
May our happiness never end.
You are the love that lights my way.
You delight me with everything that you say.
You make me feel totally right.
May our love always shine bright.

Ben Miller
Elkhart, IN

Death

Of all the things to cheer about
It's the end of life I can do without.
Remembering the righteous deeds
done in my youth,
and hoping they are
a good excuse
that the grim reaper would gladly take
before he comes to end my wake.
It's not the end of life that's sad,
but the death of all the dreams I've never had.

Mitchell Dailey
Pittsburg, CA

Hello to everyone who loves poetry. My name is Mitchel Dailey and I am married to a lovely wife named Viola. We have been together for thirty-eight years now and have two sons who also live here in Pittsburg, CA. I have a book that I read constantly called the Treasury of American Poetry. All the poems in the book were selected by Nancy Sullivan who is also a poet. My poems are about life and all the facts that are associated with it. Thank you very much for selecting my poem "Death."

The Inner Voice

I hear you speaking,
I know not from where,
I hear you calling me, and I fear.

Entrapped in mind and body, I submit.
A way of life for me to live.
My inner voice at once compels.
My soul cries out, "What is this hell!"

I fear, I grieve.
Alone and lost.
The temple of my soul entrust.
The agony of my twisted self,
Cannot fulfill the peace within.
To me, this nonsense is best ignored.
But this mystique benevolence, I implore.

Where once on earth my soul took flight,
Now darkness overshadows light.
Hidden secrets cloud my life.
No inner peace within my soul,
To the Heavens it unfolds,
Whereupon my grave, a story told.

Genevieve Chevrez
Simi Valley, CA

The Pelican

His walk's kind of awkward,
We all would agree,
But to see him soar,
Is something to see!

He flies so high
In the blue sky above,
Then dives for his dinner
To find what he loves.

He looks so majestic
As he glides in the air,
He also looks funny,
But please do not stare.

For there is a reason
He has such a big beak,
And those long, gangly wings,
And those clumsy big feet.

God wanted him different,
To stand out from the rest.
Maybe God was thinking,
"This one's the best!"

Donna Butland
Englewood, FL

Lovers of Hate

Hate! Hate! Hate is dangerous on Earth.
Haters love hating, and hate to retreat.
Retreating could be an answer to hate.
They, the haters swing happily and intrigue.

Who hates you, but who is dumb, and
Cantankerous haters do not have feelings.
And that is hate; the haters are doomed.
They, the haters nod, mope, and are fakes.

Keeping up with haters may be tiring.
Ideally they could practice loving;
To squeeze tingles, but ecstasy in sighing.
They, the haters feel occupational modelers.

Who cares to care for the haters?
We know that haters are carelessly aimless.
And we hope the Almighty one day alters,
Them, and their attitude and glee at last.
Objectively haters trade en route to hating;
Subjectively lovers always succumb to the hating.
Both are differently geared to things and arching.
They, the haters, are as unfriendly as the winters.

Cyprian Anyanwu
Philadelphia, PA

I migrated from Biafra Nigeria in 1963 to USA. Igboman's nature voyaged me several states on buses, mingling, observing people of all races, sexes, creed and ages, focusing on their interactability. Blacks found it extremely impossible to interact with another, appearing as "I hate/dislike you" written on their unfriendly faces. I observed caucasians appeared friendly regardless of strangeness—interactability was common among them. Behaviors were noticed on streets/public places. I concluded, how could blacks be hateful to themselves so melancholic, considering their overtone of being tabooed by caucasians? Isn't this grotesque?

An Irish Rose

An Irish rose of loving gold.

An Irish rose who makes me
feel young and not old.

An Irish rose is a rose who
looks in your eyes and says hello.

An Irish rose is a flower
of the rich soil of Ireland
who makes you feel happy.

An Irish rose is smiling
on happy face of the mother
who loves her "children of
Gold."

Denise Pfannkuche
Chicago, IL

I have a beautiful husband named Joseph. He works for the water department in Chicago. I have two boys, Matthew and Mark. Matthew works for Walgreens and Mark works for Lowe's in Wisconsin. I started writing poems when I was in high school. I'm a housewife now. I love children very much, and I also love pets. I have two cats, Sparky, seven years old, and Angel, three years old. I also pray for people whom I care for in my family.

Getting Old

Growing old is not a lot of fun,
You take your meds by the tons.
You lose your height by inches,
And that girdle pinches.
You hair turns gray overnight,
Not to mention you lose your good eyesight.
Your shoulders stoop and your gait is slow,
You lose that youthful glow.
New dentures and glasses you have to get,
And your best companion is your pet.
Bursitis, arthritis, and all other *itis* is your bane,
You're either on a walker or a cane
People don't call you to do important things,
They think your mind has taken wings.
You rub Ben Gay morning, noon and night,
So you can send your aches and pains to flight.
Maybe we're not as fast as we used to be
But we're full of wisdom and glee.
One day you'll be in my shoes
Then you'll understand my views.
But all in all life is good;
God brought us this far like He said He would.
So count your blessings and keep on stepping
Because someone didn't make it.

Lois L. Smith
Indianapolis, IN

My inspiration for writing this poem came from having conversations with my friends and colleagues. During our friendly chats it came to me that sooner or later, we would always talk about our doctors appointments, medicines we take and all of our aches and pains. We have come to the realization that through the aging process we're still blessed to be able to laugh about it.

Reunion

Those were the happy days of summer, never knowing they would end.
We signed the faces in the yearbook, vowing forever to be friends.
We were so young and foolish, we laughed and seldom cried.
We thought we knew all about life, but didn't know how to say goodbye.

Whatever happened to Sylvia? What happened to them all?
Some live on in my memory, others I hardly knew at all.

And so I went on without them, wondering what I left behind.
I guess I always knew the answer, what's in the past is in our minds.
I'll never know just why it happened, and why they all faded away.
But sometimes I think about them, and I imagine those happy days.

Whatever happened to Sylvia? What happened to them all?
Some got invited to the party; others never knew there was a ball.

And now we're all a little older, and wiser, some might say.
The women, most had children; while the men, most had their way.
How many dreams were shattered? Or lie stranded on time's sand?
Are we happy? Well I wonder; life happens in the middle of our plans.

Whatever happened to Sylvia? What happened to them all?
How many were disappointed? And how many had it all?

And now we'll have a class reunion, how can it have been so long.
We heard different music, and did not know each other's song.
"You know I'll call!" she said. "We'll stay in touch," I replied.
It was all so reassuring, each hoping that the other had not lied.

Whatever happened to Sylvia? What happened to them all?
Whatever happened to Sylvia? Does she remember me, at all?

Patrick McCarthy
Ft. Collins, CO

One day there arrived in the mail an envelope from "Sylvia." My wife looked at it and asked, "Who is Sylvia?" Because I had no clue who "Sylvia" was and because I consider myself to be half-way smart, I suggested that she open the envelope to find out. Sylvia, as it turned out, was a high school classmate and sometimes girlfriend. She was inviting me to the only class reunion we have ever had, after thirty-five years. My response to this news was, "Whatever happened to Sylvia?" My memories sparked the words of this poem.

Those Precious Years

It is so very hard for me to say
How much I miss the joy of years gone by
When all of life was free of care, and gay.
What happened to those precious years? I sigh.
My days were full of laughter everywhere.
The house was warm and beckoned us to stay.
The loss of Dad was just too hard to bear
When sweet sixteen those days were turned to gray.
The hours of those sad days loomed dark and low
Until a ray of hope shone through the sky.
It was an image in an eerie glow
That made me think that it was not good-bye.
I then knew what would wipe away the tears:
The mem'ry of those sixteen precious years.

Jean Denning
Rancho Mirage, CA

Dear Santa

Dear Santa,
You'd think I'd ask for a truck full of gold—
Or all kinds of silver and treasure untold,
A mink or a sable and an expensive car
A trip to the Orient or someplace afar
I could ask you for many material things
Including a lot of expensive rings
I could ask you for diamonds, a house and a man
But I'll be just as happy if you bring what you can

Carol L. Mosley
Springfield, MO

I'm in a uke band "The Happy Plunkers" and a girls' dance group sponsored by the American Legion. I play music in a jam twice monthly at the senior center and do many other activities to keep me young and healthy. We entertain at nursing homes and other volunteer places and activities. I'm seventy-eight.

Contrasts

Heavenly blue skies, liquidy sunshine, carefreeness ...
Fragments of leftover summer.
Peace and tranquility reign.
Shadows on the horizon, black unbinds
Shedding a million farenheits against the skyline ...
Birds of death soaring, turning, burning.
Orange-red fire, smoky black ribbons staining the blue sky
Raining stones and grayness and body parts and misery.
God has died.
Evil lives.
Phoenix rises from the twisted grayness, steely smoke
Choking off the cries, the death-throes.
Silence, colored black and gray and filled with doom.
Then Phoenix rises from the hell on earth.
A living spirit colored blood-red and bone-white and royal blue
transcends the horror and despair.
A spirit from the living side remembering those who perished
Shimmering over smoke-filled faces and uplifted arms
And chants from the mammoth coffin ...
Life is gone, yet life goes on among the charred heroes
and the bleeding martyrs.
God lives.
Evil dies beneath the colors.

Patricia A. Carroll
Plaistow, NH

Departed

The house seems empty, cold and bare
When I enter each room—no one's there
An empty chair sits in a special spot
That our daughter so carefully and lovingly bought

The ever-changing scenery God gave us to admire
To capture this beauty was your desire
You saw beauty in an old barn, lake or tree
How you captured it on canvas was a mystery to me

The long driveway is now covered with snow
Without a strong hand the snowblower won't go
The garage door seems to have a mind of its own
If I call for help would you answer the phone?

You lived for the times you could spend with your boys
Hunting and fishing and making them toys
A little red wagon rigged with a sail
And down the street they flew if the wind didn't fail

Dune buggies for the ground, gliders for the air
Model airplanes you built with patience and care
To watch them soar and fly was truly a thrill
Alas, to crash and demolish into the hill

Dear one, time has a way of passing and the years don't last
Our time is an era soon to be in the past
Fond memories written, remembered and cherished
Will live in my heart and never perish

Faye Nichols
Sandy, UT

Purple Heart

A little purple heart, some never get to see,
But that little heart means so very much to me.
It reminds me of the battles our men so bravely fought
And paid the price for freedom,because with their lives they bought,
Freedom for our country, freedom for you, for me.

To live here in America in a democracy,
Not for lives of greed and hate, sin, and luxury,
But bonded together in peace and harmony.
To worship God as we choose, to love and honor all,
America awaken! Don't let our nation fall.

Not to be divided, but joined together as one,
Citizens arise! Now your time has come.
Remembering the past, what was done for you,
Be faithful to your country! Stand firm and see her through.
The good times and the hard times and for her to pray,
America, we love you! God bless the USA!

Janice Block
Marengo, IL

Interior Designer

The foundation is shaky, unsteady.
The walls are squeaking lies.
The arch of sturdy love is broken.
The windows of inner transparency are fogged.
The walls no longer lead within.
A blockade of dust remains.
Truth has fallen and shattered.
Broken pieces line the floor.
Fragments from the past, no longer whole.
Cupboards bare and cold.
The nourishment is gone—starved!
Lost in a frightening doorway—Hell!
No light reaches the attic corner.
Memories are piled up.
No key to fit the lock.
No protection from the cold.
You call upon the decorator
for major reconstruction.
His tools begin to drill.
The answer is created.
Another day, a new formation.
Light begins to trickle in.
Flowering plants are set to bloom.
And love takes the flight of stairs,
In two!

Sylvia Loran
San Jose, CA

Honoring Our Military

To all those who've served so gallantly
To preserve our land and liberty,
We thank and commemorate you
For the battles fought for our red, white and blue.

Oh that these past wars would forever ensure
That peace and happiness might endure,
But, with threats from terrorists all around,
Sadly, destruction and killing abound.

What a wonderful world this would be
If all could look back in history
And realize that hatred has to cease
And be replaced by love to achieve a peace.

To all those in service and combat today,
We honor you each and every day,
And thank you for keeping America strong,
And for fighting injustices so very wrong.

Martha Morrissy-Call
Downey, CA

The Star Above

However so high I catch a twinkle in my eye
A star so bright that I see, the star above whispers to me
I dream day by day as every day passes away
The star above is still there right by my side everywhere
The star above kisses me telling me to wish upon it for it will grant me
any wish

It loves me like so, it's my star to be
That star I'll name
I'll believe in it for the rest of my life to be
The star will be with me in my love within my heart
It's there if you wish on it, twinkling up high in the sky
It's there, you just have to believe
And if you wish on it my star above is there

Cassia Cleaveland
Appleton, ME

A Cruel Cycle

I want to laugh and not cry.
I want you to sing me a lullaby!
You see I have so much to give.
Please help me live!
I can make you smile if only for a little while!
Even though I am only two
I learn by example *strictly* from you!
Please let me act my age!
Do not yell at me in rage.
So many times I have tried to laugh and have fun.
I guess I am not a fortunate child.
You see me as unruly, rough and wild!
I want to be a perfect adult like you.
Become a master in all you do!
Then I will grow to be meek and mild
and eventually learn to beat my child!

Victoria A. Josephson
Melbourne, FL

Four-Letter Words

What two words have four letters,
That start with the letter "L" and end with "E"?

Both words are priceless,
Yet, neither one can be bought but, both can be sold.

You can have one and not the other,
But, it is better to have them both than neither one at all.

One is more physical and the other affection,
One has its time limit but, the other can go on forever.

Both are taken for granted, one more so than the other,
One is seen everywhere, the other sometimes you wonder.

One word is "love," that is how I feel about you,
The other is "life," and that is how long I wish to love you.

William Konjura
Orlando, FL

Poetic Tool

Poem-writing is a hobby
I take joy in doing,
As you'll see if you proceed,
In reading words ensuing,
Expressing how I feel about,
The people whom I know,
And situations I've been in,
As through this life I go.

This poem contest interests me,
It's hobby put to use,
Where I can share emotions mine,
No reason for excuse;
My soul is bared with every line,
To paper I do pen,
Without a bit of hesitance,
I so display each yen;
The zeal expounding thoughts,
Which may, for years, have been pent-up,
I pleasurably offer you,
Upon which you may sup.

So, as I reach the end of rhymes,
Fulfilling contest rules,
I hope you like the poem I've writ,
With word poetic tools.

Larry Rosenbaum
Pembroke Pines, FL

Diversity Is What Makes Us Great

Children gathered to share their poems
Some from mansions and others from mobile homes.
While we may not strongly resemble each other
Just remember we should not judge a book by its cover.
Yellow, brown, black, or white
My color doesn't determine how I write.
My words originate deep from within
They are not determined by the color of my skin
Some poems rhyme and some may seem like endless chatter
But it's the meaning of the poem not their styles that matter
Different people will write about different places
But we won't judge them by the features of their faces
Poems are written with passion and fire,
They may express your fears or deepest desire
Poems can be about many things
Like your greatest hopes or simply a summer vacation
Like our life their only limit is our imagination

Marshall Seguin
Plant City, FL

Santa Claus

I will always believe in Santa Claus
For I was told, when I was young,
Santa is a feeling
That makes you kind to one and all.
I was taught we celebrate
The greatest gift to earth.
On Christmas Day, in memory,
Of Jesus's lowly birth.
I am ever grateful,
For that wondrous gift, from Heaven,
And enjoy the message that I'll get,
And any gift I'm given.
My faith in "Santa Claus"
Has grown from year to year,
And I hope the kindness that I've received,
Has been spread to those so dear.
I send my loved-ones greetings
In this special little rhyme,
And pray God will keep you safe,
For another Christmas time!

Penny Deck
Steamboat Springs, CO

The Empty Chair

The tables were ready
The food all prepared
The guests were all seated
When I saw the empty chair

Tonight we had the dinner
That we had this time of year
But this time it was different
Because you weren't here

We try not to notice
And get on with our life
The family we knew is shattered
And nothing will be right.

We think of you often
And speak your name
But no matter how we try
The empty chair remains

We know not what the future holds
Or who the next one will be
When next we get together
How many empty chairs will we see?

Bertha Hunt
Avella, PA

Poetry

When I feel in the mood
I like to write a poem or two
It's something that comes over me
Something I should do

With all the work there is to be done
Windows to wash, vacuum to run
Clothes to mend
So many chores to attend

With beds unmade
Closets to clean
I can't unattach myself
Like reading a good magazine

The other days
I suffer no effects
No ideas come into mind
Work done, nothing's left behind

If you feel there's something
Something you would like to do
Get it done
Chores can wait, have your fun

The work won't run away
The dust will settle down
There's no prize
For the cleanest house in town

Catherine Marin
Bayside, NY

Record Never Equalled

On a farm that, white board fences show,
With rolling land, throughout will know.
And plenty of spirited horses, in there,
Some shortly galloping, others prancing where.
All contained on farm, in eastern Kentucky,
Their owners hoping, in any race be lucky.
Whether at Churchill Downs, or Belmont Stakes
Top-prize win and record, also they make.
Also maybe one day, who knows might break,
The winning time of any, colt to take.
Though doubt if any, Secretariat's record undermine,
Ran in Kentucky under two, a horse so fine.
On the mile and three-sixteenth, he did do,
A record that to date 2013, none equalled to.
One of the greatest racing horses, have known,
With speed and stamina, he has always shown.
In the seventies, triple-crowners were three,
Secretariat '73, Seattle Slew '77. Affirmed '78 be.
None since Affirmed in 1978, ever came through,
In 2012, I'll Have Another, had two, none at Belmont do.
So now in 2014, we will just wait,
To see if a triple-crowner, will make that date.

Frank Veach
Danville, IL

Then and Now

Remember when the parents would say, "Where is this old world
    going?"
When they would look at the way man was working and the wild
    seeds they were sowing
Some would laugh at the sayings and then would make jokes of what
    was being said
The old folks would have the last word in saying, "Look at the way you
    are making your bed"

Times have changed and now we are the people that have grown old
We look as if we have really battled the wind, the rain and even the
    snow
Many have said, "I wish we could go back and live like they did in the
    past"
If we could do that, you could readily see few would be able to last

Many men and women have died trying to defend what they loved the
    most
Did not matter to them if they had to go to defend it on a foreign coast
The question that we need answered as we walk in freedom down the
    street
Would we feel and react the same as they did if this task we had to
    repeat?

America is today what it is because of the people and their actions "then"
But would America be the same if this had to be repeated again?
Let us be proud and stand fast to defend our great and wonderful land
Let us be the first to say, "Yes, I will go and help take a firm stand"

Thank God for America and all that we have and enjoy each day
The beauty and the freedom that we truly have on our life's way
Let us never allow America to suffer a loss that would be hard to recover
Let us be like the hen that over her chicks she would always hover

Danny Howell
Jonesboro, GA

Degrees of Separation

We sit by the fire watching the snow fall outside and don't speak. We can see through the sliding glass door as the deer come in to the salt lick. The spotlights hit them like bullets. They jump but just slowly walk away, each in a slightly different direction. It happened to us like that but it was much less glaring, less shocking. More like the way hot fudge pours out of the pot into the pan. I throw another log into the fire as he sits in his La-Z-Boy wearing his blanket like a suit of armor. His first round of chemo was fourteen years ago, twenty-eight years into our marriage. "You can't begin to understand, you don't have cancer." The fire has died down and we head to bed hand in hand. We kiss tenderly then lie on our sides, him on his left, me on my right, backs close but not touching.

Nancy Clark
Reedsville, WV

Memories

Years go by, life is fleeting,
I still remember our first meeting,
I loved you from the very start,
I thank you for holding the key to my heart,
You are my life, my love, my very soul,
I thank you for making my life whole,
I love you more with each passing day,
You are truly loved in a special way,
Each day we share together is a treasure,
Each moment with you an absolute pleasure,
Days, weeks and years go by,
Along with our children we laugh and we cry,
It's not about the pain, frustration, and sorrow,
It's all about the memories we create today and tomorrow,
For it's those special moments that we remember,
Moments our children will cherish forever,
Be grateful and happy without even a tear,
For the family you have, you love and hold dear.

Donald Dauman
Depew, NY

I am a simple family man with an amazing wife and two terrific children. I began poetry writing as a simple yet thoughtful way to express my love and appreciation for my beautiful wife of twenty-three years. About ten years ago it was a first-time poem at Christmas that started an annual tradition. I didn't think much of it but my wife was ecstatic. Since then I write something every year!

Despair

At morn and eve I sit
In solitary pause.
Not aware of a soul apart
Hovering near.
My heart and mind are closed
To anything that pleads to me.
I sit and ponder a life,
That confounds me and torments me.
It reminds me of my uselessness,
Unable to serve as I wish.
Unable to ask God for help.
Is He out there waiting
To open the door of my heart?
I guard it with indifference.
A spirit attaches itself to me,
It pleads as I mourn.
It stands outside the walls of my soul,
And begs for admittance.
But still I feel a need
To wallow in my despair.
My eyes slowly open and I see,
A tiny flame in the darkness.
It slowly seeps into my mind,
That only love will drain
The pit of my despair.

Dona Wilson
Tucson, AZ

Treasured Moments

Sitting and chatting with my dad,
is one treasured moment I once had.

Remembering in the kitchen, how I
used to help Mom bake,
is one treasured moment, time cannot
erase.

Visiting an older person, just to see
them smile,
And to know you've made it brighter
if only for a while.

To have a friend to laugh with and sing,
And time to praise God for all
wonderful things.

These treasured moments, are but a few,
of beautiful times, that were spent with you.

Treasured moments, beautiful moments,
I'll remember all year through.

My family, my friends, God bless
all of you.

Melanie Funk
Scottsdale, AZ

The Marine

He was a lad of seventeen who dreamed of being a Marine
School diploma in hand, would Mom understand?
She did and signed a form allowing him to wear the uniform
He enlisted and was trained well before being sent into hell
With bombs and bullets flying soon he and others lie dying
Victims of an explosion incapable of detection

He was sent home in a box that was sealed, condition of his body not
    revealed
At his funeral Mom chose to quote from a letter that he wrote
"In the worst case scenario, if unexpectedly I must go,
Please Mom don't grieve, you allowed me to achieve
What had always been my goal and I am a very happy soul
I know there is a Heaven somewhere, in the future I'll see you there."

Mom was happy he had lived his dream
Now at age eighteen he will always be a
United States Marine

Jo A. Cording
Orlando, FL

Soliloquy of a Soldier

"For my country I fought,
honor, courage I sought.
On the front line I bravely stood,
armed, ready, by my comrades understood.

Awarded the highest medal, a beauty,
for service rendered beyond my duty,
my pride reached its peak,
while still an answer I seek.

A sense of despondency I harbor in my heart,
Why is my being carrying an onus so tart?
While I reminisce my days of glory
I try to make sense of my sad story.

I've fought, I've killed the enemy unknown,
undefeated advancing, toward bloodshed prone.
But where is my true, well-deserved award,
as I've failed in my attempt to better the world?

An eye for an eye, a tooth for a tooth,
was I truly a hero, or a heartless brute?
My victorious achievement should make me glad,
so, why in my heart do I feel so guilty, so sad?

Benedetta Milstein
Buffalo, MO

My name is Benedetta Milstein. Born in Europe, I've always nurtured a love for writing, such as poetry, essays, short stories and proverbs. My thoughts go to all soldiers in the world, ours in particular, whether for a good cause or not. A soldier will be wounded if not physically, emotionally for sure, or both. I thank and honor all our men and women who face a conflict. Are we truly prepared to lend a helping hand, physically and emotionally, to our heroes and heroines?

The Postage Stamp

Did you ever stop to think
How it helps in many ways
This handy piece of paper
That's a part of all our days?

Without a thought about it
You lick it and you stick it
Giving it the importance
Of a first class ticket.

It can travel just next door
Or a thousand miles away
Carrying all its secrets
For the same amount of pay.

Its cargo is just endless
Too numerous to mention
Considered one of the world's
Truly great inventions.

What would we do without it?
The thought is really scary
To find a substitution
We'd need a magic fairy.

So give this tiny messenger
The credit it is due
And hope that in the future
They'll have a tastier glue.

Marilyn Golly
Mesa, AZ

Untitled

Along the road to Morristown
As I travel in the night
I pass the towns of small renown
Who haven't got there quite

Their founders thought
So long ago
We'll build a city don't you know
A town of wide appeal

We'll bring in settlers
From the west
Go east young man's the cry

Our townsmen
Will be of the best
Of derring-do or die

Oh what has become
Of the master plan
Prosperity has gone by us
It must be that the zoning ban
Conspired to deny us

I wave to them
As I pass in the night
But darkness there is creeping

I wave to them
As I pass in the night
They don't because they're sleeping

Donald J. Squire
Somerville, NJ

Homemaker's Lament

How peaceful the night when all are asleep,
I sit alone with hours at my feet.
As if a queen in reign,
I'm on a make-believe throne
to read, to write, to meditate,
a choice exclusively my own.
How easy decisions can all be made
a soft musical background is an added feature
and a wonderful aid.
The cares of the day slowly dissolve
and the chores for tomorrow begin to revolve.
Not one interruption, a doorbell, or telephone ring
What perfect bliss this is—my midnight fling!
The muted bark of a dog from the distance is heard
and presently, as the first faint ray of dawn appears
the birds begin to sing forth
their early morning cheers
and finally, with the fatal peal of an alarm,
down the stairs comes my family
with all their "resounding" charm.
Now you may think this silly
'cause I lost a good night's sleep,
but being "Me" for a while
was something that just couldn't keep.

Betty J. Kudirka
Beecher, IL

Fight Pattern

Day after day, the pattern's the same:
Smack dab right over our house
They drone and they roar, shake window and door
And frighten our resident mouse.
The first time I heard them, I ran to the yard.
(We'd been here an hour or two.)
I first saw three, then four and five
As larger and louder they grew.
I shaded my eyes and gazed in real awe,
Amazed at the ease and the grace
That the camouflaged planes stayed aloft in the sky,
And my joy must have shown on my face.
I don't run so quick now but still thrill to the sight
Of the Air Force planes winging by.
Sometimes I watch 'til they sink behind trees,
Whether it's daylight or night.
Sometimes I fancy they see me down here
And wonder if they see my face.
I smile, and I wave and wish them all well
As they go home to Pope Air Force Base.

Doris S. Waddell
Albemarle, NC

*I was born in Cameron, NC on March 1, 1925. After graduating in 1943,
I moved to Baltimore, MD and began writing poetry. In 1946 I married
Theodore Lee Waddell (Ted) and we had four children. We lived in
Albemarle, NC until our children were grown, then returned "down home"
to the Sandhills. After the oldest son's near-fatal automobile accident in the
1960s, I began making notes on a calendar, which later expanded into a
journal. Following my husband's death in 2009, I returned to Albemarle
where I currently reside and continue to journal.*

Blessed Baby Vaughn

I was blessed with a brother,
a baby brother named Vaughn.
He weighed seven pounds,
and came out with a frown,
but healthy as a cow.

Each moment with Vaughn is so much fun,
he means so much to me.
I like to hold and feed him,
I like his quirky sounds.
I like to play each and every day,
for one day he'll be my age.

He toots and scoots and sometimes poops,
but that's what babies do.
I even change him once a day,
'cause I know he'd do the same.

I'm just so happy to have him,
life wouldn't be the same without him.
I thank my mom and I thank my dad
each and every day for my baby brother Vaughn.

Gavin Blore
Lebanon, OH

In third grade all students were to write and read a poem in front of parents and other classmates. I was inspired to write "Blessed Baby Vaughn," because of all the love I have for my new baby brother.

Mother's Day Tribute

Mom, you were a fine lady
your face filled with character.
A smile with real sincerity that
shone like purest gold.
Graying hair like a silver crown.
Such tenderness in your eyes,
the beauty in your face like a perfect rose.
With love your arms held me close.
You taught me to remember ...
the flowers not the weeds
sunshine not the rain
life's pleasures not the pain
prayers answered, wishes fulfilled.
So on this Mother's Day and as
all the days gone by ...
thoughts of you bring me
happiness of all the cherished
memories.

Margaret M. McBride
Ashland, WI

Loss

the telephone rings
suddenly the room goes still
with a tinge of gray, hovering
sadness is an empty swing,
a single rose, a broken wing
all of these, I see, and
images, like figures on a silver screen
reach out to me—
outside, the poplar leaves are falling.
gently falling, one by one
or more, love, the core
as I watch them fall
like sweet discarded dreams
they nestle in tall grass below
the poplar leaves, now giving in
—the poplar, letting go—

Bobbie Morris
Swarthmore, PA

To Remember

Sitting on the porch; I sit, listening.
In the distance, I hear dogs, cars, people
shouting; the normal sounds of life.
Behind me? A small, white house is full of
different sounds. Sounds of four small feet.
As I look to my right; looking through the
screen door, I see two small children, smiling;
proud they found me—when I wasn't lost at all.
Coming to the door, their mother hurries, but
relaxes, and smiles, when all she sees is me.
Once upon a time, it was her tiny feet I chased,
my daughter and my son, doing the same things
her babies do now. Rocking once more, I smile,
I listen, and I remember.

Cathy Henry
Adrian, GA

*My name is Catherine Henry. I was born June 1, 1951 to Harold and Leota
Bassham. I have a brother, Richard Bassham, and a sister, Sandra Ogden.
My children are Kent Redd and Amanda Roe. My son-in-law is Sgt. Ryan
Roe. The two adorable subjects of my poem are Kate, four years old and
Alex, eighteen months. The two keep me mentally and physically active day
to day wondering what they may decide to do next.*

Mother

Once when I was very small
Just about three feet tall
You were my comfort, security, and friend
How I wished those days would never end
But as I grew, it became quite clear
I had to be more independent and that caused some fear
As time endured
I was self-assured
You would always be there when I needed you
And you are still my friend too!

Janet Colello
Castro Valley, CA

Untitled

I need more time—
    to hold you close to me
    and remember all that used
                to be.
I need more time
    the days are short when
    there is no sun.
    No dreams to share with
                only one.
I need more time—
                stay a little longer—

Doris Levenson
Delray Beach, FL

Play for Us, Minstrel!

There came a man dressed in scarlet gay
To whom the villagers called out to say,
"Play for us, Minstrel, of things far away!"

Stroking the purple feather upon his cap,
The blonde man sat and laid a lute in his lap!
"Of far away things I might sing of mayhap."

Villagers, young and old, gathered 'round
For to hear his lute to make a merry sound!
"Play for us, Minstrel, for surely tales abound!"

Nimble fingers touched the strings thin
As he sat upon the wooden storage bin.
"I may sing of a king with a malevolent grin."

In the crowd, women with much care
To the man they approached with eyes aflare!
"Play for us, Minstrel, of knights and maidens fair!"

The young minstrel strummed the thin strings
And the melodic sound of the lute sings!
"Ah, I may sing of knights who fight in the rings!"

Many an eager young lad agreed before
The women objected to the genre of gore!
"Play for us, Minstrel, of battles and bloody war!"

The minstrel strummed tunes of the lute he bore,
And he looked towards the crowd once more.
"Fear not! I'll sing much before the night's o'er!"

Heidi Ann Hildebrandt
New Richmond, WI

My skill for writing poetry is a gift from God. Also I inherited my love for poetry's musical words from my Mom who composes gospel and kids' Bible songs. Growing up though, I hated reading, writing, and memorizing poetry. Then back in 2011, I read poems by Tolkien, Poe, and Tennyson and decided I wanted to do that. Since 2011, I've written over thirty poems. "Play for Us, Minstrel," I wrote in 2012 after hearing a lute play a medieval song. With God's help, I hope to compose more poetic tales.

Untitled

A beautiful glass has
broken, we shall
drink from it no more.
We will reach and get another, but from
this glass we shall drink no more.
We remember the happy days, the sad
days, the smiles, the tears, the first cup
of coffee, so many things.
A beautiful glass has broken, we shall
drink from it no more.
We will go to the future, we will see
the sunrises and we will see the sunsets.
We will see the children grow, enjoying
the wonders of this world.
For all of this, thank you God.
A beautiful glass has broken, we shall
drink from it no more.
The shattered pieces lie on the floor
but let us look up at how fortunate we
are to have held such a beautiful glass.
Thank you for this.
A beautiful glass has broken, we shall
drink from it no more.

Paul Cristafard
Dania Beach, FL

*I have written thirteen poems. This poem was the last so far. One night I
woke up at 2 a.m., and this came to me, written in twenty minutes.*

Dearest Sweet Mommy

I used to watch you go to work
everyday
Taking care of white babies and their
families
Many late nights and weekends
without a complaint!
I wish you could have stayed home
You did what you had to do for your
children
You even made breakfast for us
before you went to work
I remember my friends saying our
mothers don't do that
I love you very much!
My special mother and black queen!

Nancy Davis Hunt
Brooklyn, NY

I am a black wife and mother of one precious son Kasiem, and I have a grandson, Joshua, and granddaughter, Jessika. My brother Buddy and sister Nina were blessed to have a father who is deceased in our lives. I am blessed by God with my gift of writing poetry. I love to help anyone who is in need. My mother worked from age fourteen from North Carolina to New York City to Baltimore, MD, retiring from domestic work at age eighty. She instilled love, faith, hard work, and the importance of getting the best education. She is ninety-one years young and lives in Baltimore on her own.

Sunset

The sinking sun suspended
  in hovering haze,
Slowly slides behind the hill
  where he sleeps until the dawn.

Diane Clay
San Marcos, TX

I am a sixty-two-year old woman born in Dallas, TX. I wrote this poem when I was eighteen years old. My childhood piano teacher was driving us to her vacation home located in the Ozark Mountains in Arkansas. As we were driving down the highway, I was admiring a beautiful sunset. Later, I was taking a creative writing class in lieu of freshman English in college. We were studying haikus. Although my poem is not a true haiku as far as having three lines of five, seven, and five syllables each, it does have a subject matter of "nature."

In August

In August my heart did sink,
In August did my confidence shrink.
This is a message that is honest and true.
I've never had anybody hurt me like you.
Your heart seemed to glimmer and your smile did gleam.
You seemed nice, funny, compassionate, and sweet to me.
Those were lies and it was but a dream,
But in reality you were vindictive, controlling and mean.
You'd only take care of me to lead on my heart,
So in the end you'd manipulate it like art.
You ripped away at my heartstrings by every seam.
You played my heart everyday,
And I loved you, but I thought that it was okay,
But autumn came, and you never talked to me again.
Not a word, but I told myself this is the end then.
My heart is still healing from your wicked way,
But I learned to never let anybody hurt me again in this way.
My heart is guarded, and my walls are built to last.
My wall will come down when prince charming can help me forget my
    past.
I'm waiting for true love that will last,
But I learned something very valuable from you,
That I'll never get hurt by anyone untrue.

Jacqueline Baglio
Norton, MA

Vintage Hankies

A tisket, a tasket,
hankies in a basket—
solid colors, plain-edged or with lace,
ivy twining or a carved pumpkin face,
cabbage roses or morning glories,
kittens dressed in overalls tell their stories,
forget-me-nots or purple pansies,
days of the week that are dandies,
four-leaf clovers or interlocking hearts,
Christmas trees or the Queen of Tarts,
white daisies or embroidered initials,
Fleur-de-lis or Scottish thistles.
Vintage handkerchiefs were once done up with care
just like one's cotton underwear—
laundered, dried, and pressed just-so,
hankies were a necessity to go.
For wiping away tears or a runny nose,
cleaning glasses or binding a stumped toe,
a handkerchief became a dolly too
to keep a child quiet in the pew.
Hankies were thought of as genteel
to care for life's necessities, if you will.
Replaced by modern paper tissue,
hankies are now a forgotten issue.

Judy Russell
Hartford, KY

The Worm and the Snail

A worm and snail were headin' different ways
The worm was crawlin' along, towards his home
A lovely spring day, on paths through the grasses
The snail was inchin' for home, from a roam

Unknown to each other, their routes would meet
In distance, neither had far, to go
And both shared a travelin' trait
Their only pace, was very slow

As the day passed, both strove on
Just before dark, was when they met
At a cross-trail, their journey ended
There they collided—they had a wreck

They both survived, and both agreed
When asked about the accident facts
We're not quite sure. It's all just a blur
It all happened so lightning fast.

Duane Williams
Durango, CO

Roaring Twenties

Roaring twenties
Into the arms of my parents
I arrived
Bouncing, laughing, doing what all babies do.
Into the land of bobbed hair
Cute little cloches
Buster Brown haircuts as
knees appeared above the new skirts.
Prohibition
Speakeasies
Bootleg spirits
FEDS
Mountain stills
Model T cars
Rumble seats
The new era began—
Leaving forever the gay '90s behind.

Loraine Storck
Waukesha, WI

Age as an old wine—mellow. I was raised in a mother-intensive household, without even a washing machine, and walked a mile to school. It was a time of simple pleasures followed by a world-wide depression and then a devastating world-wide war. I married, of course, had four children boomers—two of each—and subsequently sent all of them to college ... including courses for myself. I worked in several law firms and finally in a physician's office—primarily to pay my son's medical bills from cardiac surgery. Then I followed up with world traveling—the bug bit hard. Now I am retired and find time to do poetry.

My Visitor

You came to visit me last night
And sat on the side of my bed.
Your hand softly brushed my cheek,
No words needed to be said.

You know just how much I miss you
And still can't believe you are gone.
But with a smile and a touch of my hand
You promised I would never be alone.

I know you are always beside me,
I feel it in my heart.
But the days and nights get more lonely
Each day we are apart.

I pray each night to join you,
But you tell me I need to wait.
That I have things to do and places to go,
And you will be waiting for me by the gate.

Joyce Vice
Lufkin, TX

Life

When you are young
Life's just begun
As you grow older
You know you've won

The years go slowly by
You wish that they would speed
So you would grow up fast
So you could take the lead

Mom and Dad know nothing
They are no help to you
Then all at once you realize
You miss all that they do

As you leave home you feel
Just a little sad
What lies ahead for me?
I hope it's nothing bad

When your hair turns silver
You know what lies ahead
The years will soon be golden
As you toddle off to bed

Kayla Kimball
Blue Earth, MN

My Wisconsin

Wisconsin has always been my home,
I really like it come rain, sleet or snow.
Right off you must be really tough,
for sure the weather can be equally rough.
With rolling hills and lakes galore,
you can find a bit of Heaven along Lake Michigan's shore.
The people you'll find are great to know,
They will give you a hand, come rain, sleet or snow.
I've been to Florida, Arizona, and more,
But always come back to Lake Michigan's shore.
Hunting and fishing has been my thing,
Wisconsin provided this, feels like a dream.
If in the forest or on the water,
You'll find Wisconsin gives more than a quarter.
Am I happy and content,
without a doubt, I have to say yes.
I could go on and count the ways,
but in Wisconsin I intend to stay.

Melvin Mrotek
Oak Creek, WI

Sunrise

I like to sit at early dawn
And watch the rising sun,
As it comes o'er the mountain top
To start it's daily run.

And there I sit and concentrate
On God's great love so grand,
Who made it possible for me
To live in this fair land.

It gives me courage for the day
To do the best I can,
And to complete, ere comes the night,
The task that is at hand.

And when at last the day is o'er
And labor then is done,
I thank my God for rest at night,
And for the rising sun.

Helen Hanson
Smyrna, GA

Touchable, Mapped, and Mine

He stirs next to me
the covers dipping down his back

Hair splayed over the pillow
a halo,
encircling his ageless face
in a golden glow

Eyes—now cracked open
revealing clear blue skies
glossed over
by the clouds of sleep

Lips—a pale pink
thin, yet full,
turned upwards, ever most slightly
as he gazes across my face

Skin—flushed
and freckled, and flawed
perfect and smooth, yet ever so real
touchable, mapped,
and mine

Surreal—the dazed god beside me
returning the same love
I give to him

He is here,
lying next to me
and he is so beautiful

Bianca Buschor
Melbourne, FL

Love

Oh my the skies are so beautiful
Like you
Like you
The ocean is so wary
Like you
Like you
Skies are so big and small
Like you
Like you
Trees are so green and blue
Like you
Like you
Days are so tall
Like you
Like you
Birds are so fluttery, so exciting
Like you
Like you
Love is so deep and lasting
Like you
Like you

Melba Jane McKnight
New Castle, IN

Untitled

Lift every toilet seat
When in a public restroom
By careful maneuvering of your toe.

A restroom's a retreat
And for some it's like a womb,
Where way too many people like to go;

And don't touch the doorknob
Where every errant finger
Transfers disgusting goo that starts to grow,

And where there'll be a gob
In which the germs still linger.
So make your exit using an elbow.

Steve Talbert
Fairfield, CA

Love

Love is only a four-letter word and is
the sweetest word that's ever been heard!

Love is God, who loves us all; and he will
give us strength to stand tall whatever
befalls our day; our God will make a way.

Love is to forgive as long as
you live!

Love is doing a good deed by giving to
someone in need!

Love is the smile of a little child!

Love is giving your time that money cannot
buy; only patience can apply!

Love is from the beginning of time
Love is a gift that is yours and mine!
Love will last to the end of time!

Cornelia Tolbert
St. Louis, MO

Soft Secret

Clouds are magnificent, easy to see
Clouds each different never alike
Soaring high, higher breathtaking
Painting the sky floating clouds
Soft secret ... hidden high.

Wind blowing gently morning clouds high
Painting perfect patterns images to see
Eyes closed darkness, silhouette I see
High above, higher soft secret ... hidden high.
Harps play, soft music clouds dance
Bump, bump, careful clouds dance
Spin, dizzy I feel free, music above
Soft cotton, white puff, puff I blow
Lifting clouds oh no!
Please pattern do not disturb
Clouds painting the sky, soaring high
What do clouds hide high?
What are secrets clouds conceal?
Soft secret, soft clouds, secret care garden
Heaven is hidden made for
You and I!

Khoda Stone
Louisville, KY

I am an expressive creator. Poetry is an enigma with words that fit into our minds. Poetry is the heart, a language and real-life events that can reach out and touch anyone. I think of poetry as a literacy explosion of the human heart!

The Orphan

I looked into the child's eyes
They were big and they were wide,
But there were hollows of sadness
Buried deep inside.

She was longing for affection,
A hug, a kiss, or word so kind,
To ease the pain she felt
Coursing through her mind.

She is now a grown-up woman,
Still wondering how it'd be
A happy, carefree little girl,
Sitting on her daddy's knee.

To have had kind, loving parents,
Who wished her all the best,
Who tucked her into bed at night,
Where she'd enjoy contented rest.

Bonnie E. Virag
Novi, MI

The inspiration for my poem "The Orphan" came from my book The
Stovepipe. *The book is a memoir and tells the story of my life and that of my
sisters as we were snatched from our home at a tender age, separated, and
raised in several foster homes. It is a story of sisterly love and our triumph over
adversity. The Stovepipe has received a Kirkus Review "Star," awarded to
books of considerable merit, and selected as a Kirkus Review's Best of 2012.*

Untitled

Oh, sweet child with eyes that shine,
So much like one that once was mine.
What can I say? How can I share it.
Things I know of the world you'll inherit.
I know one day I will go away
But with my children and you, part of me will stay
For in the plan of all creation,
our genes are passed to each generation.
I'm not sure you'll think that's terrific,
But, I hope what I leave won't be just scientific.
Oh, sweet child with eyes that shine,
So much like one that once was mine.
I want you to know how much I love you,
How proud I am of you.
I want you to go through life with strength and pride.
With the power of God by your side.
But with a heart full of joy and love,
For your fellow man, the earth and skies above.
I know some day, you'll hold a baby and say,
Oh, sweet child with eyes that shine so much like one
that once was mine.
What can I say—How can I share it?
Things I know of the world you'll inherit.

Nancy Krueger
Rockford, IL

His Heart

Two hearts that joined—soon became one;
The sorrow started, over was the fun.
We laughed, we honored, we cherished, we cared—
Each precious moment these two hearts shared.

And so it was over—without a good-bye;
No use to suffer, no need to cry.
The darkness came, the silence fell
And no longer my true love would tell.

His mouth was closed—his eyes were shut;
He would never tell what—
Two hearts had done and gone wrong—
Now this heart sings a very sad song.

This song will be new—never heard before,
A smiling face one always wore;
The other frowning, worthless grin—
It seems one heart could never sin.

Diane C. Parzygnat
Newnan, GA

Diane is a native of Atlanta, GA and a graduate of Georgia State University. As an eight-year cancer survivor, she currently writes poetry for healing, therapy and enjoyment and to reach new milestones along the spiritual journey. She lives South of Atlanta with husband, Andy, and enjoys time with her ninety-year-old mom and only sister, Beverly, who lives close by. Hobbies are loving life and people, and a great extended family in Chicago.

Ruminations

As inevitable as our next breath,
is the certainty of our death.
Why not, therefore, enjoy this life
instead of filling it with strife.
Let peace and joy forever reign,
anathema to sadness, pessimism and pain.
With but one life to live,
let us not only take but give.
If a friend acts in a manner kyphotic,
why respond or act neurotic.
Never forget life is a precious gift,
permit it to give us a lift.
Take time to smell a flower,
or from the sea, experience its power.

Patrick N. Hart
St. George, UT

Loneliness

Loneliness
no hope
no future
but wanting
Pain
never ending
mind numbing
but reminding
Life
a journey
a reason
but lost
Love
sometimes healing
sometimes real
but not for me

Larry Garner
Alleman, IA

A Tribute to the Survivors of the Holocaust

The Holocaust, the epitome of man's inhumanity to man,
An inconceivable event in history; the master plan.
Born of a demented, diabolically warped, crazed mind,
Whose raving, cruel demand surpasses that of any other kind,
And led an entire nation through the very gates of Hell,
Bringing utter and complete disgrace to all mankind as well!
Consider the plight of these victims, father, mother, son and daughter,
Herded together like so many innocent lambs heading for slaughter,
Plundered, confused, abused, insulted, degraded, robbed of will,
Starved and reduced to mere skeletons with no blood left to spill!
But then, an added, final act of shame, with regret unremitted,
Like so many animals; upon their arms tattooed numbers imprinted!
Work camps, death camps, gas chambers, furnaces, in Faustian revel,
Could a crueler scenario have been envisioned even by the devil?
What was left for these devastated victims to hope for or endure?
Sensing that much of the world had turned a blind eye for sure!
A journey into an inconceivable dimension of hopelessness and shame,
Wondering upon what possible dire crime lay the cause of their blame?
Where, thought some, was their God when they needed Him most?
Could He too have turned the other way unmindful of their satanic host?
Where was there a single ray of hope to grant them the slightest light,
Of some tiny, miniscule pinpoint of a very distant star that might,
Grant them the merest chance of rescue from this maddened nation,
To once again live free, in safety, with dignity befitting their station?
And yet, as impossible as it was to envision, some did manage to survive,
Proving to the world that against all odds, this noble race was still alive!
And here, today, at this Holocaust museum site, that once mark-of-shame,
The tattoo, has been transformed into a mark of honor without blame!
Within my breast there still persists a burning rage which flames
ofttimes,
To think that mankind was given to commit against mankind such
crimes.

Ludwig Savarese
Deerfield Beach, FL

Untitled

Customers
can be big or tall
little or small

Have brown, yellow or blue
hair. Who really cares?

A customer is a human being.
You don't judge them in any means.

They have humor. They have
grace. They're the best in any race.

You'll find a friend in your customers
listen to what they have to say.
They'll understand you're there for
them anyway.

My customers make me smile,
laugh and even joke. That makes
them the best of folks.

Janet K. Jackson
Huntingburg, IN

I have a big family, eight brothers and six sisters. My mom passed away April 18, 2013. The poem I wrote for her about Wednesday. People told me they loved it, or should I say most of my customers said that. She inspired me and so did my customers. I miss my mom so much. It's my customers that keep me going. I have a pizza place called Brick Oven Pizza. I run it through the day and my husband runs it at night. If I'm not working there, I take care of my dogs. I love my dogs more than anything. That's my life.

Words

I am unequivocally perplexed

As to who formed words
And why they could wound someone
So torturously
And make them ache in agony and
Snivel despairingly into the dying night
With a feeble moon veiled behind closed eyelids;

As to what happens to words when
You die, full of beauty and mourning
And where they go or if they stay or if their implications
Contain the same type of necessary resolve
A word can hold in a world with limited time,
Or if the voices declaring them
Have the same naïve sound,
A sound of ignorant corruption;

As to how, in all my life,
I have been drowning in a ghastly sea
Of words that ravage and destroy and mend
Softly woven, gentle hearts
And have not encountered a single word
To describe the remarkably strong, fervently curious essence
Of you.

Misako Yamazaki
Phoenix, AZ

*My name is Misako and I have a passion for writing, reading, and music.
My inspiration to begin writing began with my love for the Harry Potter
books written by J.K. Rowling. Currently, I am sixteen years old and my
goal is to have my first book published by the time I turn twenty-one years of
age. I love poetry, young adult literature, and Shakespeare. As for my poem,
"Words," I have always been fascinated by the power words can hold.
Words, all a combination of twenty-six letters, can wound as well as repair
someone for better or worse.*

Bird-Watching in My Kitchen

When it's morning in my kitchen,
A bit of spring is there.
For the call of the recipe soon fills the air.
Calling clearly for clarified butter, half-a-cup.
Or dispirited for lukewarm water, mix-it up.
The true recipe gives a light lilting lisp,
When it calls for a third of a T. or tsp.
From a nest of mixing bowls, one hears the stirring,
Of the great wooden spoon or a small mixer whirring.
And the grease is flying in a flock
Of spatters toward the kitchen clock.

At noon, standing quietly in disguise,
One can watch the souffle rise.
Close by, in cool green leafy bower,
The crusted croutons crouch and cower.
And if your sight is keen and patience great,
You'll see a crumb alight your plate.
Though crumbs are common, hardly rare,
(They're in my kitchen everywhere)
It is a treat to see
Them settle where they ought to be.

As night falls softly on my domain,
I hear the gurgle of the drain.
Then, only mournful motors moan,
No daytime sights or sounds remain,
But I am not alone,
For something old, something sad
Is resting on my Brillo pad.

Reba G. Krehbiel
Columbia, MO

My family consists of three sons, Curt, Bruce, and Les, and my husband and myself. I wrote the poem because I have spent part of my whole life in the kitchen. Make that several kitchens, a smallest kitchen in Wokott-Wood Drive, a larger kitchen on Parkdale Blvd, and one larger than all my kitchens off of Creasy Springs Road.

Joan Marie

The winds of March come
flowing by to raise our
kites into the sky

The April rains wash them
The last of winter's blustery day

The flowers bloom, the robins sing
Nature smiles and welcomes spring

Then summer comes and wind is
warm, bright sunny days, then
thunderstorms, that wash the
earth with welcome rain
I watch with wonder through my
windowpane.

The days turn cool, the leaves fall
down, spreading color on the ground.

I watch the changes with wondering eyes
the days of summer have flown by.

The first snow falls, the air is still
with winter frost and crispy chill.
The days are grey, the Earth is white,
the nights so clear with stars so bright.
Time seems to slow the season's change
but I know spring will come again.

John V. Payne
Douglasville, GA

A Deer's Life

A mother deer and her fawn
play and eat in the grass without
any sorrow.
Little did they know they could
be gone by tomorrow.
Shot by a hunter's gun so they can
call it fun.
Tan of color and small white
spots, a beautiful sight shining
in the sun.
Playing without a care, but
time is running sun.
Playing without a care, but
time is running out.
What would the world be
like if they were not about!

Millie Illmensee
Colts Neck, NJ

Flowers in Spring

Flowers in Spring
are a beautiful thing.
Reds, purples, and blues,
they're all different hues!
But the one that I love,
is as white as a dove.
A daisy, you see,
is the flower for me!

Tricia Combs
Walnut, KS

Affirmative Anticipation

Your greatest asset is you
Good ideas belong to everyone
Every person is unique, so celebrate
We all have potential ability

Every day, try to be extraordinary
Stretch beyond the common
Live a day at a time
Hold onto hope

Doris Calkins
Rock Rapids, IA

Diary of an Arrowhead

Indian women chipped me
Indian men shot me
The rabbit outran me
The archer could not find me
Trees sheltered me
Wind exposed me
Sand covered me
Rain washed me
Cactus protected me
Snow chilled me
Fire scorched me
Hail pelted me
Deer trampled me
Humans hiked on me
Rivers carried me
Years aged me
You found me
I was not broken and neither was my spirit

Chrissy Watkins
St. George, UT

I will never forget the night I wrote this poem. I love to look for arrowheads or petroglyphs or pottery, anything Indian related. This one evening, I found a beautiful white bird or rabbit point. I went home and went to bed but couldn't sleep, couldn't get this poem out of my head, I knew I was being inspired. My rough draft was actually written on a paper towel, the words just flowed. This is the only poem I have written. My thoughts were the hope that the deceased Indian who shot this point knew how much I loved him and the arrowhead.

A Gift

To you, whose mind like giant tentacles
Reaches out to grasp unlimited knowledge,
And pursues truth with unquenching thirst,
To you, were it mine, I would give wisdom.

To you, whose anguished soul searches for meaning,
And seeks the infinite hope of something unseen,
Questioning, searching, yet never understanding,
To you, were it mine, I would give faith.

To you, whose body is shackled and confined
Because of the ignorance of man,
A product of a cold and unyielding justice,
To you, were it mine, I would give freedom.

To you, whose body aches for the touch and
Tenderness of a gentle hand,
The whisper of a soft sigh, the nearness of silent lips,
To you, were it mine, I would give love.

Wanda M. Ross
Port Orange, FL

Flames

If you could look into my heart
I'm sure that you would find
A fire burning brightly warm,
gentle, sweet and kind.

You're a tender—sweet, gentle and
true man, warm gentle—sweet and kind.
No other in this world, kisses give
ecstacy like this.

With raging flames of tenderness
that kindle, when we kiss,
no other fuel and all this—world
gives ecstacy like this.

For if the fire should ever die,
and fate should be unkind,
my world would turn to ashes and
my heart would lose its mind.

Barbara Gault
Mencelona, MI

I live in Northern Michigan, not far from Jordan River. I have been writing poem since the age of ten. I like all poetry. I wrote this poem for my sons Richard and Jaime, also my partner of twenty-seven years, Clint. They have always had faith in me.

Summer Evening Breeze

Sitting on the front porch watching cars pass by
Counting all the colors and catching butterflies
Running through the grass barefoot and free,
That summer evening breeze, chasing after me.

Planting all the flowers and climbing up the trees
Grandma's good cookin', it's instilled in me.

And though you're not with me,
Your memory still is.
Always in my heart, forever you will live.

You taught me how to work hard, use my hands and mind.
Whistle through the day's work, one song at a time.

Strong-willed and determined, you worked hard to stay alive.
I can still smell that saw dust, it makes me cry every time I
Feel that summer evening breeze catching up to me.

And though you're not with me,
Your memory still is.
Always in my heart, forever you will live oh,
That summer evening breeze, it caught up to me.

And it takes me back
It takes me back
To a simpler time and place of those sweet, sweet summer days,
Those sweet, sweet summer days of my childhood days.

Your voice, it is a melody, forever always playing,
Through that summer evening breeze.

Kelley Club
Simpsonville, SC

293

Yesterday

Yesterday was just us two
Yesterday was me and you
Yesterday, yesterday
Is no more

Yesterday the sun was bright
Yesterday things seemed so right
Yesterday, yesterday
Is no more

Yesterday would last forever
Yesterday parting was never
Yesterday, yesterday
Is no more

Yesterday would never end
Life and love with my best friend
Yesterday, yesterday
Is no more

Yesterday we two had fun
Yesterday we two were one
Yesterday, yesterday
Is no more

Jack Marquis
Arcata, CA

When Jewel my wife of over fifty-four years passed on, the loss was utter devastation. This poem was my way of trying to cope with the reality and pay respect to a very special lady.

Untitled

Lost, dazed
confused, alone

seeking shelter
from the unknown ...

Twisted, turned.
wounded, burned.

Hurt, crushed.
delivered, rushed.

Tears flow
slowly down
steady stream to the ground.

Tears stop
falling down
stop tears.

Smile appears
fake or real.
dry my eyes
from wet tears

keep going
find me
keep going
over here.

lost, dazed
confused, alone.
seeking shelter
from the unknown.

Stacey Winters
Magna, UT

Sweet Lady Kinsey

Sweet Lady Kinsey
My precious collie rescue;
A beautiful girl eight years old.

You needed me and I needed you;
My precious companion
Always by my side—
Unconditional love abounds!

Not big on treats
But loved our walks
Sniffing the trails ...
Watching the birds.

Riding in the car like a queen
So well behaved
You were the best!

Always at the door
When I came home
You welcomed me
with pure love and joy!

My guardian angel of the night
Resting on the floor by my bed.

When cancer stole you
It broke my heart!
You gave me your best four years.
My sweet lady—Kinsey

Ruth A. Fishero
Westerville, OH

My inspiration for this poem came because of my collie name Kinsey. I adopted her from a collie rescue when she was eight years old. She and I were the best of friends. It broke my heart last year when she got bladder cancer at the age of twelve. I miss her terribly! I am a widow, a senior citizen and live by myself. I have three children, nine grandchildren and twelve great-grandchildren. I am so blessed! I grew up on a farm where we worked hard. Life was of a slower pace back then and families enjoyed Sunday together.

The Lights of Lurray

I looked down from a mountaintop of Skyland, VA
and I saw the lights—the lights of Luray.

Luray, Virginia, what a beautiful town!
So quiet, so peaceful, so sleepy, so sound.
I listened as one sang of your beauty up here
as your bright lights twinkled in the dark night so clear.

I came down from the mountain at the break of day
and I saw the sun rise over Luray.

The bright sparkling lights of the night were all gone
and the singer had finished singing his song.
Still in my mind's eye, I can picture it here.
That sweet summer night is ever so near!

Sandra Rodness
Minneapolis, MN

Ants, Ants, and Circumstance

How do you like your ants?
In the house, in the plants
Everywhere they roam
Throughout the nooks and crannies
Of every single home.

Smash them on the steps
Chase them out the door
They find their little ways
around your each and every floor.

Take them outside
Let them ride your foot piggyback
Only you must never, ever
Let them come back.

Worst of all
Don't let them loose
To crawl inside your shoes.

Ants, ants, and circumstance
They just are
In the house, bed
And probably your brand new car.

We have to get rid of these pesky beasts
So stomp them each and all
But you'd better beware
When their armies come to call.

Instead of ants, ants, and circumstance
Look out for ants in your pants!

Karen S. Odom
DeKalb, IL

I Saw Jesus

Since we are all God's children
And strive for our heavenly home,
We are to see God in everyone,
Be it strangers, friend or foe
And to strike out at anyone
Would he striking God himself.

The comparison I could not understand,
The angry young man who defied the law,
The lost young woman who chose the wrong road,
The politicians who cheated and lied,
The exhausted laborers who lost all hope,
None appeared god-like to me.

But my hospice patient, although near death
Smiled weakly in spite of pain
With peaceful and accepting eyes
Struggled to recite my name.
Death, as life, can be an effort
But God's help sees us through,
And I believe I saw Jesus today.

Rita Sharon
Escanoha, MI

It's What's Become of Me

I used to soar with eagles, my spirit was so free
But now my life is sadness, it's what's become of me

It's a burden I must carry, in my heart and in my soul
My life was changed forever, the day you had to go

It's a long road I must travel, a lifelong journey it seems
Whatever happiness I am given, is only in my dreams

Sometimes it weighs heavy on me, other times it lets me be
It's the life that I've been dealt, I can never be set free

I carry this burden bravely, because I love you so
My life was changed forever, the day you had to go

My emotions get so high, and then can be so low
My heart feels like it will never heal, because I love you so

At times my heart's so full of joy, I think, how can this be
Sometimes I'm up, sometimes I'm down, it's what's become of me

Laura Corkill Broussard
Lafayette, LA

My maiden name is Laura Corkill. I was born in San Diego in 1954 but currently reside in Louisiana. I have always loved to write my thoughts, mostly when things are going bad in my life. It's therapy for me. I was married at eighteen and had two sons. The inspiration for this writing was my youngest son Jayson who died at the age of twenty-three. He was a great person with a big heart and a friend to all. His passing changed my whole world. I have three grandchildren now who fill my heart with joy. Love you, Jayson.

Berlin Wall 1990: The Fall

The faces ... expressions to never forget
Euphoria unmatched, I have seen now
Hands clasping, hearts trusting, acquaintance renewed
The world looking on and wondering: "How?"

The wall of severance has finally come down
I saw old men weeping, old wounds cleansed with tears
"Why didn't this happen sooner?" they said,
"Dispelling the hate and death through the years"

A preponderance of stone to be bought and sold
Enterprise moves in to stake her claim
I wondered which stones were stained with blood
To souvenir seekers, they all looked the same

Reunification of Germany now
The ghosts of the past looking on
The heinous rock gone from its perch
Never forgotten but finally gone

Men of small minds with chips on your shoulders
The Berlin Wall is no more to be
Your dreams of detainment are nothing but boulders
Historically now ... East people are free ...

Evelyn Shriner
Lawton, OK

Two Words

There are two words that everyone likes to hear
And they never change from year to year.
My grandparents said them and so did Mom and Dad
And they told me about them when I was a lad
Always say, "Thank You," when someone gives
To you:
Such as a present, a good deed, or a kind word, too.
"Pass the french fries please," you ask at dinner.
Then, you say, "Thank you," and you are a winner.
"I like your haircut," a friend might say.
"Thank You," is your reply, each and every day.
It is a sign of respect and don't ever forget:
The more you give, the more you get.

Bob Breslo
Rio Verde, AZ

I'd Like a Salad

I'd like a salad, oh yes I would
I'd like a salad, but please if you could
Hold the lettuce and spinach
Hold the cucumbers and cheese
Hold the mushrooms and olives
Hold the nuts if you please
Hold the carrots and ranch
Hold the sprouts and tomato
Hold the meat and the peppers
Hold the avocado
Hold the croutons and onion
Hold the sunflower seeds
Hold the hard-boiled egg
Hold the radish and peas
Basically I want a bowl with a spoon
But I'm getting hungry so please bring it soon

Hailey Nicole Bzdok
St. Cloud, MN

I have recently turned eighteen and I am pursuing a career in accounting. My other passions include theater, making collages, and poetry. I have participated in four musicals, made a miscellaneous collage that is over seven feet by ten feet and is still growing, and have been writing since elementary school. Famous poet, Shel Silverstein, has inspired me for years to write off-the-wall poetry. Some of it may not make complete sense, but I like to think it is entertaining for all ages.

Life Forward

Open your eyes, ears, mind and
Heart to conform in making of
The right decision in life forward
State of confidence to be
Happy; only to see the sun
Shining to transcend our
Mind full of enjoyment as to
Say, "OMG," have a nice day.
OMG is also to mean give
Generously, so that it can
Be given to those that seemly
Seems unfair to understand
The circumstances that led to
Know their needs are critical.
So it is that we need to take a
pause, relax, be refreshed and
Look out yonder to see life
Forward is spinning faster
Than a locomotive to take
You where? New York; yes,
There are many that stands
On the street; you'll hear a
Song, "Can you spare a change" dollar.

Tadashi D. Kiyabu
Ewa Beach, HI

My Friend Died

She went away
One day
We used to play
As children
We played all day
Life went by
I want to cry
She went away
Old and grey
She went away
I miss her everyday
She went away
Somewhere
That I can't see
Not yet anyway
She went away
To a place that is
Far away
And she will stay
Until the day
I go away
And then we will play
And laugh and be
Happy on that day
No more going away
My friend and I
She didn't die
She just went away

Arlene B. Young-Fleig
Tallahassee, FL

Born January 19, 1934, in Boston, MA, I am an artist, poet, wife, mother, and nana. I worked at Harvard University under Dr. Roy Gordon in the chemistry department doing research and other interesting duties as well. My first poem was published in 1986 in the Lamoille County News, *Morrisville, VT. I am in the process of writing a children's book about a family of centipedes who come to live with us. Oil paintings shown by appointment only, this poem was inspired by the death of my dear friend Claire.*

Be Still

Striving to be
what you are not,
urged relentlessly for invincibility,
the stark truth you fail to see.
You are all puff: a roarless wonder.

Behold a simple lesson many fail
to glean: move towards what you
want; not away from feelings you
seek to avoid!

Black or white, red or yellow ... man!
Heed the truth that sets you free!
"Alone with God you are a majority!"

W. J. Maresca
Rochester, NY

The Homeless Ones

You see them wandering in the streets.
You see them hiding back in the dark,
surviving the freezing rain and the brutal heat
as they look for some infested corner to call home.
What secrets do they carry in their minds as
their heart beats on?
Some say they are evil, crazy, their minds gone,
the streets filled with the homeless ones.
Are they someone's parent, a friend or a daughter and son?
Are their memories just a figment of their imagination?
Do they think, do they have feelings?
Do they even know that the wet torn box and the
shopping cart they call home are not real?
If you give them a chance and just be kind,
these people could be your test or a sign.
That homeless person you did find: is she or he
really from the divine?

Donna M. Rice
Simpsonville, SC

Winter's Call

Do you feel the cold wind blowing through the trees?
I do. It is winter's call. Do you see the birds sitting on the bare limbs
Swaying in the cold breeze? They know what is to be.
My breath is like clouds floating on air, but just for a moment.
My ears sting from the cold wind dancing around them.
The leaves fall from the trees but with grace that only winter can
    provide.
It is winter's call, a call we must all answer.
As I walk among the leaves they provide a tune that only winter
    can provide.
The sky is grey like wool, but not as warm. It is winter's call, calling us
    all.

Clifford Jeli
Lehigh Acres, FL

Please Adore Me

Please adore me, I will dream big for my first kiss.
Because I love you. I sang a song it was beautiful.
I love you all day long sweet, sweet love.
I adore you on our first kiss, we would sweet-talk all day long.

Aidan Hall
Gilbert, AZ

Little Moments

Bright sun beats down this early afternoon.
Dry, yellowed grass lays flat like the back of an old horse.
Shiny black crow boys "echo-squawk" through
   the palest blue expanse of sky.
Young translucent grape leaves gently sway
   in natures slight breeze,
   seemingly straining to reach the Heavens.
Chorus of wind chimes sound there melodies.
Busy bees flit about from flower to flower ...
   a hello, then a goodbye ...
A private plane soars above,
   mimicking those same little garden bees,
So goes the life of a retiree ... me!

Nancy West
Hayward, CA

Nature inspires me. I take the time to stop and look around me. These moments to myself make me happy. My hope would be that this little "ditty" will do the same for whomever reads it. Take the time for yourself. Observe with awe. I dedicate my poem to my wonderful son, Erik, a budding young wordsmith.

Soul Mate

Almond-shaped, ocean-blue eyes gaze intently into my own.

Those eyes which read my every mood, sensing my hurts and
unfulfilled dreams blink slowly, sensuously,
reassuring me of his unfailing trust and devotion.

Praying my time on earth precedes his own—the very thought of life
without his presence, too unbearable to contemplate.

Evening comes—couch time for all. Channel surfing and papers to sort.
His head seeks my lap and I adjust my position for his comfort.

Bedtime—the day's final ritual.
Ice water in my red cup at my bedside table. Several sips languidly
      enjoyed.
Comforter turned down, pillows puffed, blankets adjusted, lights out.

His sleek, well-muscled body molds into the curves of my own—two
spoons in one space, breathing in synchronicity.

A sudden twitch, as he chases his dream mouse.
Bet you already guessed he wasn't my spouse
but my siamese-tabby forever soul mate, Smokey Joe.

Maureen Opal
Fountain Hills, AZ

Window on My World

I just looked out the window
It took my breath away
Though I had many chores to do
Something made me stay.

Across the verdant fairways
Beyond the towering trees
The mountains stood in glory
It brought me to my knees.

Sunlight kissed the flowers
The dewdrops brightly glistening
Birds were chirping softly
They knew that I was listening.

Reading on the patio
Was the man I love
Oh so many blessings
For me—from God above.

It suddenly came over me
What a lovely life
Great-grandma, grandma, mother
And a long time wife.

What's outside your window?
Take the time to see
You too can have this feeling
It just happened to me.

Barbara Fink
Rancho Mirage, CA

Rain Dance

I love to hear the little rain
Dancing on my windowpane
Pitter pat so soft and sweet
Like little goblins dancing feet

Sometimes I awake in the middle of the night
And hear you dancing with all your might
But when I awaken in the morn
I find that your dances have been adjourned

If God made you and God made me and gave us
"Breath of life"
Then the world should turn and see
That rain is "man's delight."

Donna J. Hall
Sutherlin, OR

The "Fudge" and "Noodle" Lady

I have had many "kudos"
  re my "fudge" but now
  hear my "noodles" too
        are great,
And I have proof of this
  because at Thanksgiving
  "Maddie," "Megan" and "Nikki" ate and
        ate and ate.
But girls, please hold back
  a little next time, and
  let "G-Dad" eat his fill,
Otherwise, your Christmas
  gifts may be going to
  "The Noodle Lady" in the
  "Y-Bridge City" of Zanesville!

Wanda F. Welker
Zanesville, OH

The Rose

It's only a tiny rosebud, a flower of God's
design,
but I cannot unfold the petals with these
clumsy hands of mine.
The secret of unfolding flowers is not
known to such as I.
The flower of God opens so sweetly, in my
hands would fade and die.
If I cannot unfold a rosebud, this flower of
God's design,
then how can I think I have the wisdom to
unfold this life of mine?
So, I'll trust Him for His leading each
moment of every day.
I'll look to Him for His guidance each step of
the pilgrim way,
for the pathway that lies ever before me, my
heavenly Father knows
I'll trust Him to unfold the moments just as
He unfolds the rose.

Arlene Robinson
San Bernard, CA

Night Stalker

Stealthy prowler of the night
Stalking prey in the dim light
Waiting downwind in the brush
Crouching, seeming not to rush
Which hapless victim will you choose?
Which fearsome weapon will you use?

Does boredom send you on the prowl
Or lonesome call of the barn owl?
Does instinct start you on your quest
Or hunger make you raid the nest?
Has mouse upset you scuttling around?
Has frog invaded your playground?
Has squirrel strayed too close to home?
Has opossum hung around too long?

Stealthy prowler of the night
Stalking prey in the dim light
Pupils wide and eyes agleam
Gaze affixed like laser beam
Which hapless victim did you choose?
Which fearsome weapon did you use?

Mary A. Gervin
Albany, GA

Tears of Heaven

We haven't officially been introduced,
But I love you with every ounce already.
And though this was shocking news,
I'm so excited to be your newborn baby.
I have been counting and praying.
I can't wait for you to take me home.

I know my time is not yet here,
But why are they opening you?
Why on your face is a tear?
What are they about to do?
Wait, what is happening?
Why are they laying you down?

Mama, Mama, save me!
They are hurting me!
That terrible machine!
Mama, why aren't you doing something?!

When I opened my eyes,
I was laying at God's feet.
Jesus, with the angels,
was weeping over me.
In that moment, I knew.
For alone in your room,
I saw you weeping, too.

Caitlin M. Harbin
Mobile, AL

Feeling Alone This Dark Night

Feeling alone on this night that is so dark
The pitiful man comes around, trying to make his mark
Though slight comfort comes from his words and company
And though he believes he has come with great empathy
Sympathy is all he can give to my grief
For he knows not how I feel, though that is his belief
Abandonment and betrayal are out of his reach
He does not recognize the fear that I keep
The man may believe his life is hard
But my feelings are unbelievable, for he is not scarred
How could he know, how could he find out?
Pain is a feeling he knows nothing about
This pain does not show on the outside nor
Does it come from any blood or gore
This pain is on the inside and does not go away
It stabs the heart deeper with every given day
How can anyone understand me?
The words going through my mind could mark me as crazy
How can I express this terror in a word?
For each person would say it's absurd
And my fear is that the current pain that comes,
Is not the worst and not close to being done
So I thank you sir for trying your hardest
But no one can save me from my fears and my thoughts
Just leave me here, don't remember my sight
Leave me here feeling alone this dark night

Rebecca Nicole Miller
Puyallup, WA

Just Reach Out

Reach out your hand
And pull me in closer
Take me away from
The fear and the fright
It may sound cheesy
And it may seem wrong
You might believe me

Listen to my song
Take the words
That I am saying
Hear them ring clear
Tell me you hear me
Say you understand
But I know you are lying

Hands reach toward each other
But you just let me fall
Please just tell me why
You just watched me cry

Now I am stronger
You will never win
Time will always tell
Just how I survived
Your torture and your strain

Lyndsie Ruth Bernard
Plantation, FL

A Drug with Teeth and a Pulse

You like to quote dead writers when
I ask you about your drinking.
"I do it to make other people more
interesting."
You're a regular Hemingway.
The lights in your eyes are like the
street lamps on my lane—
they only come on after dark,
when we two are on your roof,
reading aloud sonnets and waiting
to watch the sun peel away husks of the moon.

Your breath always smells like
cigarettes and licorice,
and I don't like it (I don't like licorice),
but it's okay,
because I like you.
And I wonder if you actually like me or if
you just keep me around to listen to you ramble
on about grammar and
constellations and coffee beans.

I don't know what I'd feel if that were the case, but I think
I'd feel like a cartoon
who's lost her will to be animated.

Rennie Svirnovskiy
Chesterfield, MO

Your Poor Mother

I'll bet rainy days are hard for your mother,
And I'll bet sunny days are hard too,
'Cause I'll bet every day she thinks of you.

As if my hurt isn't great enough,
My grief for her grows with every thought;
Between letting go and holding on, she's caught.
If I could do your mother only one favor,
I would carve my chest wide open,
And stop her in the midst of her failed coping.

I would tear out my heart and place it in her palms
Because it is in my heart that you reside,
It is there that you are still alive.

Brittainy Huff Pollock
Millville, NJ

Poet's Heart

Beneath a starry veil I rest
Fully laid upon the plain;
Gazing up at lighted crest,
Ears fixed on Heaven's strain.
A dreamer's dream floats like a cloud
And hovers in the balmy air.
The viol plays the solemn sound
To complete the harmonized pair.
But, like all that is a dream,
The cloud swiftly drifts apart.
The last note played at day's first gleam,
Then sinks my burdened heart.

Adam J. Roberts
Nebraska City, NE

Down and Out

Scarf it all down,
and puke it all up.
Some say it's a curse,
but I say it's luck.
Too bad I value the pearls.
Too bad I wanna hurl.

My throat's always sore.
Even my bile's chanting soar!
"Do you want some more?"
Mommy's asking by the door.

I'll never say no,
with knees pressed to the ground,
a head bent so low.

"Oh hello again."
I'd greet the porcelain
and heave all of the mistakes
that taste so sweet
that Mommy always bakes.

Ayana Caines
San Tan Valley, AZ

Escorts

You gave me a second chance of life,
currency, not exist
owe you all,
my renaissance to the east,
sun sets west,
every breath from now till ever,
red pedals fall at your feet
sweat, drop, down,
bowing my head,
my wings will spread,
my heart will guard
for you I die,
and still I'll owe!

Maciej Walkowiak
Port Washington, NY

Rejected Dreams

In a place nearly a million miles or so,
To a land where almost no man will go,
Is an isle of rejected dreams.
Full of thought and ideas,
Never followed dreams, and the hopes thought to be pointless.
Cast away, thrown out, rejected, disregarded,
As though they never existed in the first place.
They lay there waiting, vivid, bright, and bold,
Though in need of a good polish.
And when stumbled upon now and then,
They drive insane the most strong and intelligent men.
For their heads are full of rules crisp and clear,
And far too strict for this wonderful place.
A place of imagination, creation, rejuvenation, exclamation.
We are too tainted for these pure ideas.
We're taught to just toss them.
So they'll wait for what shall never come,
A person that'll accept, just for once,
The unbelievable, wonderful, unacceptable truth.
And for that, these thoughts, ideas, and dreams
Shall wait forevermore.

Yasmin Jarik
Overland Park, KS

Awakenings

As I kneel down by the hospital bed,
I lower the rail and touch her head,
Her snow-white hair and translucent skin
reveal her age, and the time she's been an angel on earth

Her eyes are open: they're pale and blue,
she's looking at something distant and true
A subtle smile, a peaceful look, a vacant stare,
it makes me wonder, "Are you there?"

Let me hold your hand so you will know
that you are loved and we all care.
 Let us guide you on your way,
until we meet again someday.

As I look up from my hospital bed,
a hand reaches down to touch my head
A face so kind and caring is looking at me ...
No, she's staring.

Is that a tear in your eye? Please don't cry.
I've had a wonderful life here on earth,
now it's time to move on
to life's final stage after birth.

I'm trying to speak, but the words won't form ...
Please understand, my hands are cold, but my heart is warm.
From inside this body, my soul reaches out—
my Heavenly Father is call me now.

Thanks for holding my hand and trying to understand ...
Thanks for your care and your tears,
and most of all, thank you so much for holding me, dear.
Goodbye, for now ...

Lydia Ray
Fairfield, PA

Index of Poets

T

Taitt, Lynn Marie 23
Talbert, Steve 275
Tarvin, Bob 86
Teixeira, Antonio P. 48
Thevenot, Janet 51
Tolbert, Cornelia 276
Tomlinson, Carolyn 64
Tommasi, Daniel 129
Trobaugh, Kenneth 187
Truax, June R. 113
Tsougarakis, Kira 65
Turner, Wanda Carol 45

U

Uta, Adele 49

V

Van Zile, Judy M. 215
Vance, Carole 93
Veach, Frank 244
Vice, Joyce 269
Vierra, Kaitlyn 198
Virag, Bonnie E. 278
Vollbrecht, Denise A. 111

W

Waddell, Doris S. 255
Wagner, Nancy 148
Walker, Timeka 35
Walkowiak, Maciej 323
Wallace, Beth 138
Wasinger, Jake 66
Waters, Richard 152
Watkins, Chrissy 290
Welker, Wanda F. 313
Wells, Helen J. 32
Wentz, Lorrian 94
West, Nancy 309
Whisman, Tara 123

Whyel, Lenia 112
Wichman, Wyatt 60
Wilkinson, Carol 199
Will, Kathleen 73
Williams, Duane 267
Wilson, Dona 248
Wilson, Dylan C. 26
Wilson, Pandora L. 115
Winn, Shirley 16
Winters, Stacey 295
Woods, Keenan 182
Wooten, Aron 104

Y

Yamazaki, Misako 285
Yeager, Kitty 196
Young-Fleig, Arlene B. 305

CPSIA information can be obtained at www.ICGtesting.com
Printed in the USA
BVOW01s0336121113

335806BV00011B/1/P

9 781608 802777